Gifts from a Jar

Cookies & Muffins

Gift Giving Made Easy

*S*how your friends and family just how much you care by giving them a beautiful homemade gift jar filled with the ingredients to bake delicious cookies, bars, muffins and scones.

Keep the following tips in mind when preparing your gift jars.

- Always use a food-safe jar or container with an airtight lid. Make sure the jar or container is completely dry before filling it with ingredients.

- Use the jar size called for in the recipe.

- Measure all the ingredients accurately.

- For ease in filling, use a wide-mouth jar if possible. Layer the ingredients into the jar using a ¼-cup dry measuring cup or the largest spoon that fits through the mouth of the jar.

- For more attractive jars, divide ingredients with large amounts (1 cup or more) into 2 layers.

- Fine ingredients such as flour and granulated sugar are best layered on the bottom of the jar, or on top of more compact ingredients, such as oats and brown sugar. When placed on top of loosely layered ingredients, such as chocolate chips or nuts, flour and granulated sugar tend to cover up those loosely layered ingredients.

- After the jar is filled make sure to replace the lid securely. Then, tear out the corresponding gift tag from this book. Cover the top of the jar with a 9- or 10-inch circle of fabric. Tie the fabric and the gift tag onto the jar with raffia, ribbon, satin cord, string, yarn or lace.

Cowboy Cookies Mix

1 cup all-purpose flour
1 cup uncooked old-fashioned oats
¾ cup semisweet chocolate chips
½ cup packed light brown sugar
½ cup chopped nuts
½ cup seedless and/or golden raisins
¼ cup granulated sugar
2 tablespoons unsweetened cocoa powder
½ teaspoon baking powder
¼ teaspoon baking soda

1. Layer ingredients attractively in any order into 1-quart food storage jar with tight-fitting lid. Pack ingredients down slightly before adding another layer.

2. Cover top of jar with fabric; attach gift tag with raffia or ribbon.

Makes one 1-quart jar

Cowboy Cookies

½ **cup butter, softened**
1 egg
1 teaspoon vanilla
1 jar Cowboy Cookies Mix

1. Preheat oven to 350°F. Lightly grease cookie sheets.

2. Beat butter in large bowl until smooth. Beat in egg and vanilla until blended. (Mixture may appear curdled.) Add cookie mix to butter mixture; stir until well blended.

3. Drop rounded tablespoonfuls dough 2 inches apart onto prepared cookie sheets. Bake 12 to 14 minutes or until edges are lightly browned. Remove to wire racks to cool completely.

Makes about 2½ dozen cookies

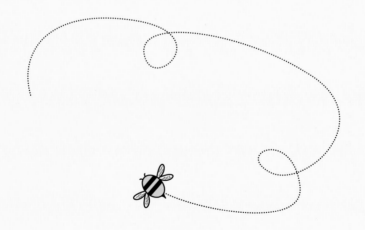

Cowboy Cookies

½ cup butter, softened   1 teaspoon vanilla
1 egg   1 jar Cowboy Cookies Mix

1. Preheat oven to 350°F. Lightly grease cookie sheets.
2. Beat butter in large bowl until smooth. Beat in egg and vanilla until blended.
(Mixture may appear curdled.) Add cookie mix to butter mixture; stir until well
blended.
3. Drop rounded tablespoonfuls dough 2 inches apart onto prepared cookie
sheets. Bake 12 to 14 minutes or until edges are lightly browned. Remove to wire
racks to cool completely.   *Makes about 2½ dozen cookies*

Cowboy Cookies

½ cup butter, softened   1 teaspoon vanilla
1 egg   1 jar Cowboy Cookies Mix

1. Preheat oven to 350°F. Lightly grease cookie sheets.
2. Beat butter in large bowl until smooth. Beat in egg and vanilla until blended.
(Mixture may appear curdled.) Add cookie mix to butter mixture; stir until well
blended.
3. Drop rounded tablespoonfuls dough 2 inches apart onto prepared cookie
sheets. Bake 12 to 14 minutes or until edges are lightly browned. Remove to wire
racks to cool completely.   *Makes about 2½ dozen cookies*

Cowboy Cookies

½ cup butter, softened   1 teaspoon vanilla
1 egg   1 jar Cowboy Cookies Mix

1. Preheat oven to 350°F. Lightly grease cookie sheets.
2. Beat butter in large bowl until smooth. Beat in egg and vanilla until blended.
(Mixture may appear curdled.) Add cookie mix to butter mixture; stir until well
blended.
3. Drop rounded tablespoonfuls dough 2 inches apart onto prepared cookie
sheets. Bake 12 to 14 minutes or until edges are lightly browned. Remove to wire
racks to cool completely.   *Makes about 2½ dozen cookies*

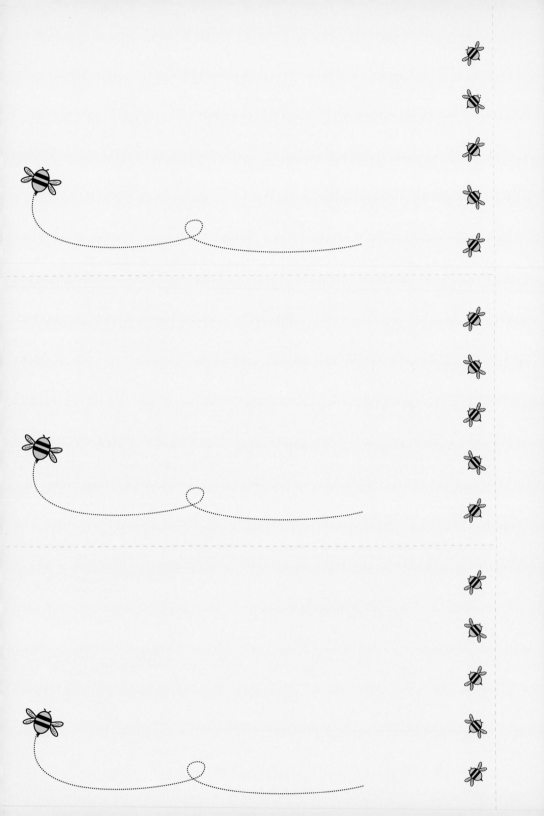

Cowboy Cookies

½ cup butter, softened   1 teaspoon vanilla
1 egg   1 jar Cowboy Cookies Mix

1. Preheat oven to 350°F. Lightly grease cookie sheets.
2. Beat butter in large bowl until smooth. Beat in egg and vanilla until blended. (Mixture may appear curdled.) Add cookie mix to butter mixture; stir until well blended.
3. Drop rounded tablespoonfuls dough 2 inches apart onto prepared cookie sheets. Bake 12 to 14 minutes or until edges are lightly browned. Remove to wire racks to cool completely. *Makes about 2½ dozen cookies*

Cowboy Cookies

½ cup butter, softened   1 teaspoon vanilla
1 egg   1 jar Cowboy Cookies Mix

1. Preheat oven to 350°F. Lightly grease cookie sheets.
2. Beat butter in large bowl until smooth. Beat in egg and vanilla until blended. (Mixture may appear curdled.) Add cookie mix to butter mixture; stir until well blended.
3. Drop rounded tablespoonfuls dough 2 inches apart onto prepared cookie sheets. Bake 12 to 14 minutes or until edges are lightly browned. Remove to wire racks to cool completely. *Makes about 2½ dozen cookies*

Cowboy Cookies

½ cup butter, softened   1 teaspoon vanilla
1 egg   1 jar Cowboy Cookies Mix

1. Preheat oven to 350°F. Lightly grease cookie sheets.
2. Beat butter in large bowl until smooth. Beat in egg and vanilla until blended. (Mixture may appear curdled.) Add cookie mix to butter mixture; stir until well blended.
3. Drop rounded tablespoonfuls dough 2 inches apart onto prepared cookie sheets. Bake 12 to 14 minutes or until edges are lightly browned. Remove to wire racks to cool completely. *Makes about 2½ dozen cookies*

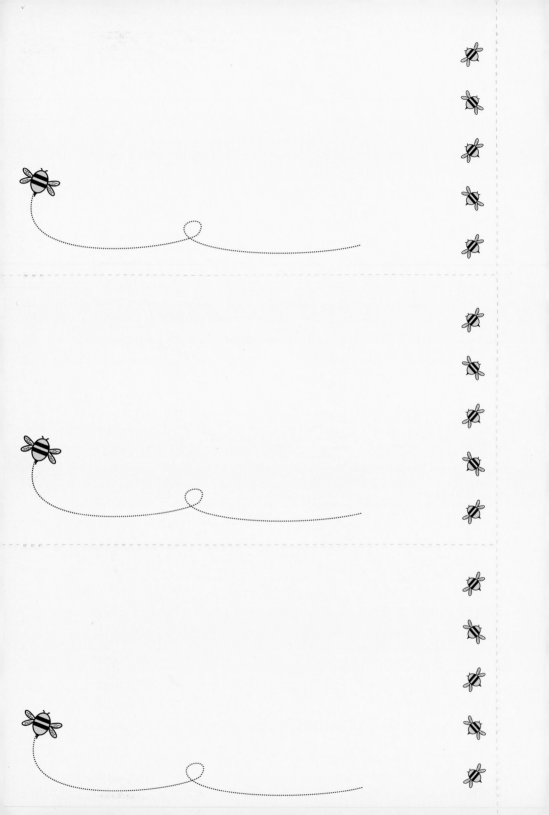

Decadent Blonde Brownies Mix

1½ cups all-purpose flour
1 package (10 ounces) semisweet chocolate chunks*
¾ cup granulated sugar
¾ cup packed light brown sugar
¾ cup coarsely chopped macadamia nuts
1 teaspoon baking powder
½ teaspoon salt

*If chocolate chunks are not available, cut 1 (10-ounce) thick chocolate candy bar into ½-inch pieces to equal 1½ cups.

1. Layer ingredients attractively in any order into 1½-quart food storage jar with tight-fitting lid. Pack ingredients down slightly before adding another layer.

2. Cover top of jar with fabric; attach gift tag with raffia or ribbon.

Makes one 1½-quart jar

Decadent Blonde Brownies

½ cup butter, softened
2 eggs
2 teaspoons vanilla
1 jar Decadent Blonde Brownies Mix

1. Preheat oven to 350°F. Lightly grease 13×9-inch baking pan.

2. Beat butter in large bowl until smooth. Beat in eggs and vanilla until blended. (Mixture may appear curdled.) Add brownie mix to butter mixture; stir until well blended.

3. Spread batter evenly in prepared pan. Bake 25 to 30 minutes or until golden brown. Cool in pan on wire rack.

Makes 2 dozen brownies

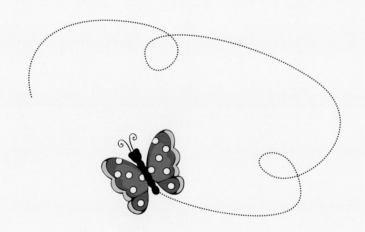

Decadent Blonde Brownies

½ cup butter, softened
2 eggs
2 teaspoons vanilla

1 jar Decadent Blonde
Brownies Mix

1. Preheat oven to 350°F. Lightly grease 13×9-inch baking pan.

2. Beat butter in large bowl until smooth. Beat in eggs and vanilla until blended. (Mixture may appear curdled.) Add brownie mix to butter mixture; stir until well blended.

3. Spread batter evenly in prepared pan. Bake 25 to 30 minutes or until golden brown. Cool in pan on wire rack. *Makes 2 dozen brownies*

Decadent Blonde Brownies

½ cup butter, softened
2 eggs
2 teaspoons vanilla

1 jar Decadent Blonde
Brownies Mix

1. Preheat oven to 350°F. Lightly grease 13×9-inch baking pan.

2. Beat butter in large bowl until smooth. Beat in eggs and vanilla until blended. (Mixture may appear curdled.) Add brownie mix to butter mixture; stir until well blended.

3. Spread batter evenly in prepared pan. Bake 25 to 30 minutes or until golden brown. Cool in pan on wire rack. *Makes 2 dozen brownies*

Decadent Blonde Brownies

½ cup butter, softened
2 eggs
2 teaspoons vanilla

1 jar Decadent Blonde
Brownies Mix

1. Preheat oven to 350°F. Lightly grease 13×9-inch baking pan.

2. Beat butter in large bowl until smooth. Beat in eggs and vanilla until blended. (Mixture may appear curdled.) Add brownie mix to butter mixture; stir until well blended.

3. Spread batter evenly in prepared pan. Bake 25 to 30 minutes or until golden brown. Cool in pan on wire rack. *Makes 2 dozen brownies*

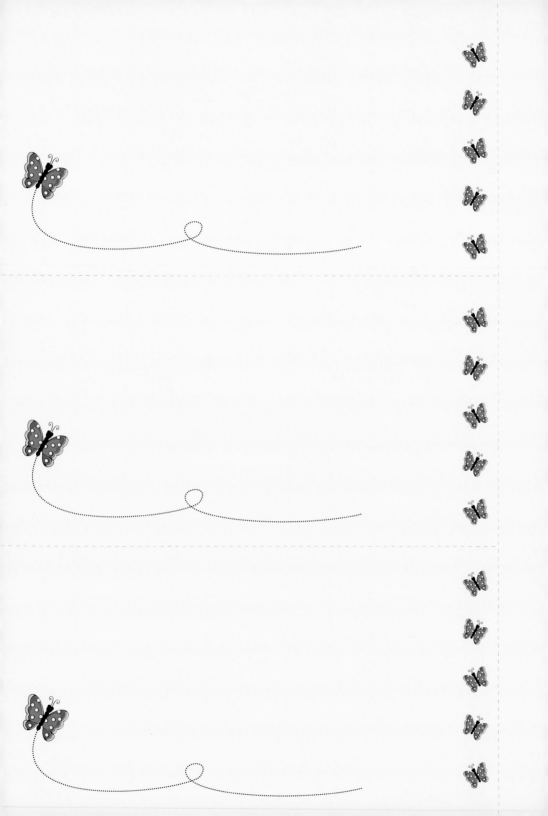

Decadent Blonde Brownies

½ cup butter, softened
2 eggs
2 teaspoons vanilla

1 jar Decadent Blonde
Brownies Mix

1. Preheat oven to 350°F. Lightly grease 13×9-inch baking pan.

2. Beat butter in large bowl until smooth. Beat in eggs and vanilla until blended. (Mixture may appear curdled.) Add brownie mix to butter mixture; stir until well blended.

3. Spread batter evenly in prepared pan. Bake 25 to 30 minutes or until golden brown. Cool in pan on wire rack.   *Makes 2 dozen brownies*

Decadent Blonde Brownies

½ cup butter, softened
2 eggs
2 teaspoons vanilla

1 jar Decadent Blonde
Brownies Mix

1. Preheat oven to 350°F. Lightly grease 13×9-inch baking pan.

2. Beat butter in large bowl until smooth. Beat in eggs and vanilla until blended. (Mixture may appear curdled.) Add brownie mix to butter mixture; stir until well blended.

3. Spread batter evenly in prepared pan. Bake 25 to 30 minutes or until golden brown. Cool in pan on wire rack.   *Makes 2 dozen brownies*

Decadent Blonde Brownies

½ cup butter, softened
2 eggs
2 teaspoons vanilla

1 jar Decadent Blonde
Brownies Mix

1. Preheat oven to 350°F. Lightly grease 13×9-inch baking pan.

2. Beat butter in large bowl until smooth. Beat in eggs and vanilla until blended. (Mixture may appear curdled.) Add brownie mix to butter mixture; stir until well blended.

3. Spread batter evenly in prepared pan. Bake 25 to 30 minutes or until golden brown. Cool in pan on wire rack.   *Makes 2 dozen brownies*

Oatmeal Raisin Cookies Mix

3 cups uncooked old-fashioned or quick oats
1 cup raisins
¾ cup granulated sugar
¾ cup all-purpose flour
¾ cup packed light brown sugar
¾ teaspoon salt
½ teaspoon baking soda
½ teaspoon ground cinnamon

1. Layer ingredients attractively in any order into 1½-quart food storage jar with tight-fitting lid. Pack ingredients down slightly before adding another layer.

2. Cover top of jar with fabric; attach gift tag with raffia or ribbon.

Makes one 1½-quart jar

Oatmeal Raisin Cookies

¾ cup butter, softened
1 egg
2 tablespoons milk
2 teaspoons vanilla
1 jar Oatmeal Raisin Cookies Mix

1. Preheat oven to 375°F. Lightly grease cookie sheets.

2. Beat butter in large bowl until smooth. Beat in egg, milk and vanilla until blended. (Mixture may appear curdled.) Add cookie mix to butter mixture; stir until well blended.

3. Drop rounded tablespoonfuls dough 2 inches apart onto prepared cookie sheets. Bake 10 to 11 minutes or until edges are golden brown. Let cookies stand on cookie sheets 2 minutes. Remove cookies to wire racks to cool completely.

Makes 3½ dozen cookies

Oatmeal Raisin Cookies

¾ cup butter, softened
1 egg
2 tablespoons milk

2 teaspoons vanilla
1 jar Oatmeal Raisin Cookies
Mix

1. Preheat oven to 375°F. Lightly grease cookie sheets.

2. Beat butter in large bowl until smooth. Beat in egg, milk and vanilla until blended. (Mixture may appear curdled.) Add cookie mix to butter mixture; stir until well blended.

3. Drop rounded tablespoonfuls dough 2 inches apart onto prepared cookie sheets. Bake 10 to 11 minutes or until edges are golden brown. Let cookies stand on cookie sheets 2 minutes. Remove cookies to wire racks to cool completely.

Makes 3½ dozen cookies

Oatmeal Raisin Cookies

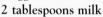

¾ cup butter, softened
1 egg
2 tablespoons milk

2 teaspoons vanilla
1 jar Oatmeal Raisin Cookies
Mix

1. Preheat oven to 375°F. Lightly grease cookie sheets.

2. Beat butter in large bowl until smooth. Beat in egg, milk and vanilla until blended. (Mixture may appear curdled.) Add cookie mix to butter mixture; stir until well blended.

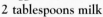

3. Drop rounded tablespoonfuls dough 2 inches apart onto prepared cookie sheets. Bake 10 to 11 minutes or until edges are golden brown. Let cookies stand on cookie sheets 2 minutes. Remove cookies to wire racks to cool completely.

Makes 3½ dozen cookies

Oatmeal Raisin Cookies

¾ cup butter, softened
1 egg
2 tablespoons milk

2 teaspoons vanilla
1 jar Oatmeal Raisin Cookies
Mix

1. Preheat oven to 375°F. Lightly grease cookie sheets.

2. Beat butter in large bowl until smooth. Beat in egg, milk and vanilla until blended. (Mixture may appear curdled.) Add cookie mix to butter mixture; stir until well blended.

3. Drop rounded tablespoonfuls dough 2 inches apart onto prepared cookie sheets. Bake 10 to 11 minutes or until edges are golden brown. Let cookies stand on cookie sheets 2 minutes. Remove cookies to wire racks to cool completely.

Makes 3½ dozen cookies

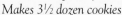

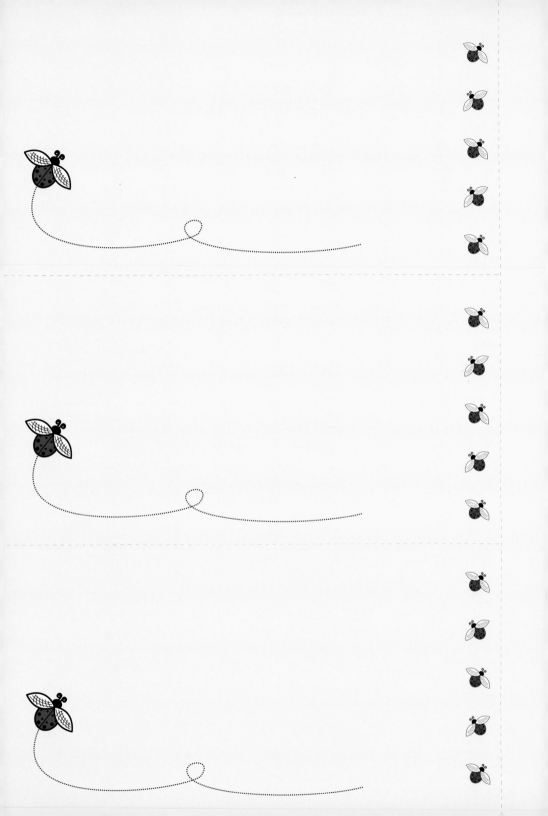

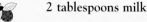

Oatmeal Raisin Cookies

¾ cup butter, softened   2 teaspoons vanilla
1 egg   1 jar Oatmeal Raisin Cookies
2 tablespoons milk   Mix

1. Preheat oven to 375°F. Lightly grease cookie sheets.

2. Beat butter in large bowl until smooth. Beat in egg, milk and vanilla until blended. (Mixture may appear curdled.) Add cookie mix to butter mixture; stir until well blended.

3. Drop rounded tablespoonfuls dough 2 inches apart onto prepared cookie sheets. Bake 10 to 11 minutes or until edges are golden brown. Let cookies stand on cookie sheets 2 minutes. Remove cookies to wire racks to cool completely.

Makes 3½ dozen cookies

Oatmeal Raisin Cookies

¾ cup butter, softened   2 teaspoons vanilla
1 egg   1 jar Oatmeal Raisin Cookies
2 tablespoons milk   Mix

1. Preheat oven to 375°F. Lightly grease cookie sheets.

2. Beat butter in large bowl until smooth. Beat in egg, milk and vanilla until blended. (Mixture may appear curdled.) Add cookie mix to butter mixture; stir until well blended.

3. Drop rounded tablespoonfuls dough 2 inches apart onto prepared cookie sheets. Bake 10 to 11 minutes or until edges are golden brown. Let cookies stand on cookie sheets 2 minutes. Remove cookies to wire racks to cool completely.

Makes 3½ dozen cookies

Oatmeal Raisin Cookies

¾ cup butter, softened   2 teaspoons vanilla
1 egg   1 jar Oatmeal Raisin Cookies
2 tablespoons milk   Mix

1. Preheat oven to 375°F. Lightly grease cookie sheets.

2. Beat butter in large bowl until smooth. Beat in egg, milk and vanilla until blended. (Mixture may appear curdled.) Add cookie mix to butter mixture; stir until well blended.

3. Drop rounded tablespoonfuls dough 2 inches apart onto prepared cookie sheets. Bake 10 to 11 minutes or until edges are golden brown. Let cookies stand on cookie sheets 2 minutes. Remove cookies to wire racks to cool completely.

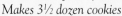

Makes 3½ dozen cookies

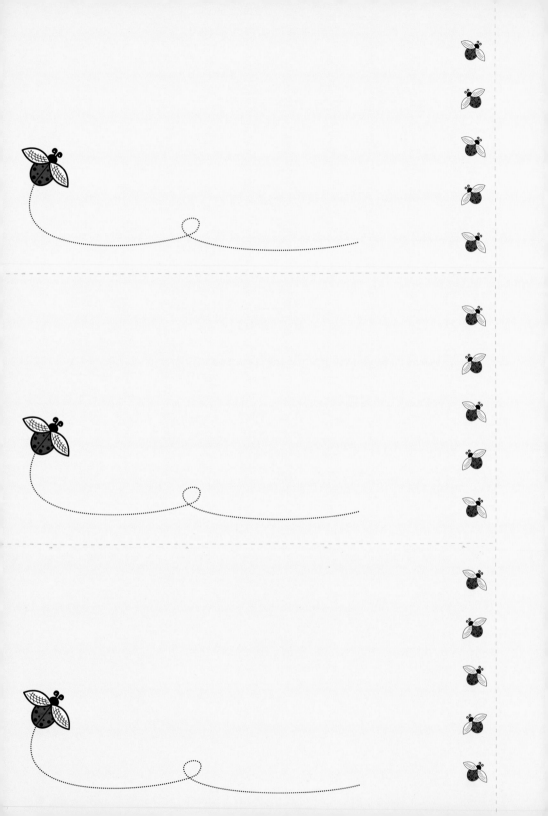

Marbled Peanut Butter Brownies Mix

2 cups all-purpose flour
1 cup packed light brown sugar
½ cup granulated sugar
½ cup coarsely chopped salted mixed nuts
2 teaspoons baking powder
⅛ teaspoon salt

1. Layer ingredients attractively in any order into 1-quart food storage jar with tight-fitting lid. Pack ingredients down slightly before adding another layer.

2. Cover top of jar with fabric; attach gift tag with raffia or ribbon.

Makes one 1-quart jar

21

Marbled Peanut Butter Brownies

½ cup butter, softened
¼ cup peanut butter
3 eggs
1 teaspoon vanilla
1 jar Marbled Peanut Butter Brownies Mix
1 cup chocolate syrup

1. Preheat oven to 350°F. Lightly grease 13×9-inch baking pan.

2. Beat butter and peanut butter in large bowl until smooth. Beat in eggs and vanilla until blended. (Mixture may appear curdled.) Add brownie mix to butter mixture; stir until well blended. (Batter will be thick.)

3. Spread half of batter evenly in prepared pan. Spread syrup over top. Spoon remaining batter over syrup; swirl with knife or spatula to create marbled effect. Bake 35 to 40 minutes or until lightly browned. Cool in pan on wire rack. *Makes 2 dozen brownies*

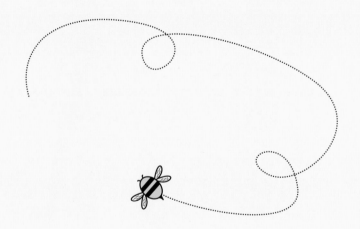

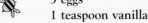

Marbled Peanut Butter Brownies

½ cup butter, softened
¼ cup peanut butter
3 eggs
1 teaspoon vanilla

1 jar Marbled Peanut Butter
    Brownies Mix
1 cup chocolate syrup

1. Preheat oven to 350°F. Lightly grease 13×9-inch baking pan.
2. Beat butter and peanut butter in large bowl until smooth. Beat in eggs and vanilla until blended. (Mixture may appear curdled.) Add brownie mix to butter mixture; stir until well blended. (Batter will be thick.)
3. Spread half of batter evenly in prepared pan. Spread syrup over top. Spoon remaining batter over syrup; swirl with knife or spatula to create marbled effect. Bake 35 to 40 minutes or until lightly browned. Cool in pan on wire rack.

Makes 2 dozen brownies

Marbled Peanut Butter Brownies

½ cup butter, softened
¼ cup peanut butter
3 eggs
1 teaspoon vanilla

1 jar Marbled Peanut Butter
    Brownies Mix
1 cup chocolate syrup

1. Preheat oven to 350°F. Lightly grease 13×9-inch baking pan.
2. Beat butter and peanut butter in large bowl until smooth. Beat in eggs and vanilla until blended. (Mixture may appear curdled.) Add brownie mix to butter mixture; stir until well blended. (Batter will be thick.)
3. Spread half of batter evenly in prepared pan. Spread syrup over top. Spoon remaining batter over syrup; swirl with knife or spatula to create marbled effect. Bake 35 to 40 minutes or until lightly browned. Cool in pan on wire rack.

Makes 2 dozen brownies

Marbled Peanut Butter Brownies

½ cup butter, softened
¼ cup peanut butter
3 eggs
1 teaspoon vanilla

1 jar Marbled Peanut Butter
    Brownies Mix
1 cup chocolate syrup

1. Preheat oven to 350°F. Lightly grease 13×9-inch baking pan.
2. Beat butter and peanut butter in large bowl until smooth. Beat in eggs and vanilla until blended. (Mixture may appear curdled.) Add brownie mix to butter mixture; stir until well blended. (Batter will be thick.)
3. Spread half of batter evenly in prepared pan. Spread syrup over top. Spoon remaining batter over syrup; swirl with knife or spatula to create marbled effect. Bake 35 to 40 minutes or until lightly browned. Cool in pan on wire rack.

Makes 2 dozen brownies

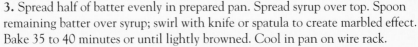

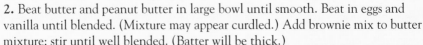

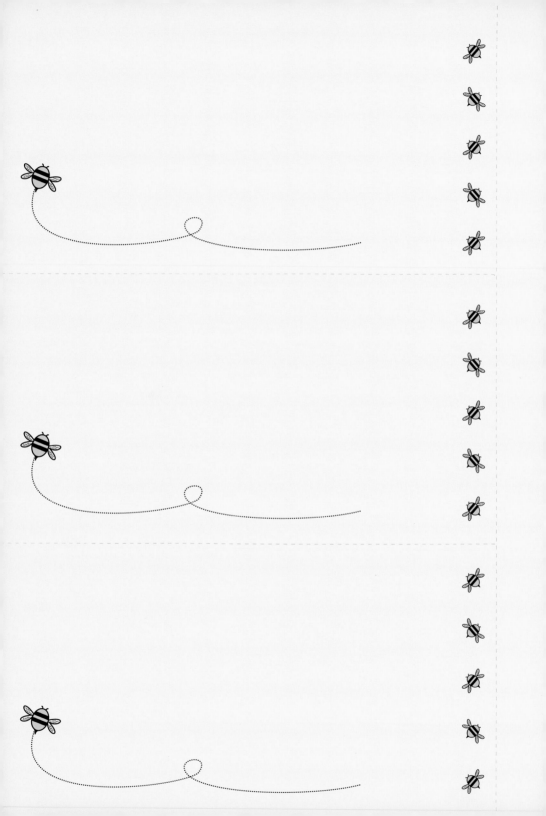

Marbled Peanut Butter Brownies

½ cup butter, softened
¼ cup peanut butter
3 eggs
1 teaspoon vanilla

1 jar Marbled Peanut Butter
Brownies Mix
1 cup chocolate syrup

1. Preheat oven to 350°F. Lightly grease 13×9-inch baking pan.
2. Beat butter and peanut butter in large bowl until smooth. Beat in eggs and vanilla until blended. (Mixture may appear curdled.) Add brownie mix to butter mixture; stir until well blended. (Batter will be thick.)
3. Spread half of batter evenly in prepared pan. Spread syrup over top. Spoon remaining batter over syrup; swirl with knife or spatula to create marbled effect. Bake 35 to 40 minutes or until lightly browned. Cool in pan on wire rack.

Makes 2 dozen brownies

Marbled Peanut Butter Brownies

½ cup butter, softened
¼ cup peanut butter
3 eggs
1 teaspoon vanilla

1 jar Marbled Peanut Butter
Brownies Mix
1 cup chocolate syrup

1. Preheat oven to 350°F. Lightly grease 13×9-inch baking pan.
2. Beat butter and peanut butter in large bowl until smooth. Beat in eggs and vanilla until blended. (Mixture may appear curdled.) Add brownie mix to butter mixture; stir until well blended. (Batter will be thick.)
3. Spread half of batter evenly in prepared pan. Spread syrup over top. Spoon remaining batter over syrup; swirl with knife or spatula to create marbled effect. Bake 35 to 40 minutes or until lightly browned. Cool in pan on wire rack.

Makes 2 dozen brownies

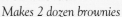

Marbled Peanut Butter Brownies

½ cup butter, softened
¼ cup peanut butter
3 eggs
1 teaspoon vanilla

1 jar Marbled Peanut Butter
Brownies Mix
1 cup chocolate syrup

1. Preheat oven to 350°F. Lightly grease 13×9-inch baking pan.
2. Beat butter and peanut butter in large bowl until smooth. Beat in eggs and vanilla until blended. (Mixture may appear curdled.) Add brownie mix to butter mixture; stir until well blended. (Batter will be thick.)
3. Spread half of batter evenly in prepared pan. Spread syrup over top. Spoon remaining batter over syrup; swirl with knife or spatula to create marbled effect. Bake 35 to 40 minutes or until lightly browned. Cool in pan on wire rack.

Makes 2 dozen brownies

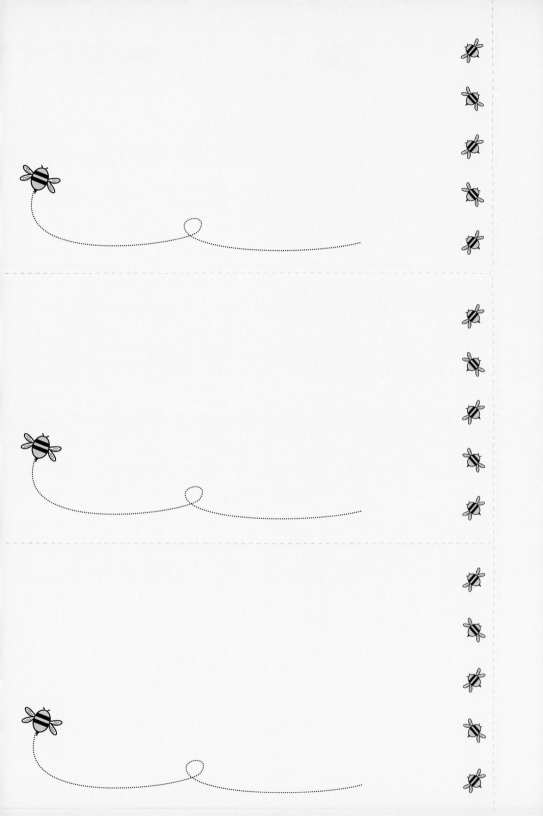

Fruit & Oat Squares Mix

2 cups all-purpose flour
2 cups uncooked quick oats
1½ cups packed light brown sugar
1 teaspoon baking soda
½ teaspoon salt
½ teaspoon ground cinnamon

1. Layer ingredients attractively in any order into 1½-quart food storage jar with tight-fitting lid. Pack ingredients down slightly before adding another layer.

2. Cover top of jar with fabric; attach gift tag with raffia or ribbon.

Makes one 1½-quart jar

Fruit & Oat Squares

1 jar Fruit & Oat Squares Mix
⅔ cup butter, softened
1½ cups apricot, cherry or other fruit flavor preserves

1. Preheat oven to 350°F. Lightly grease 13×9-inch baking pan.

2. Place bar cookie mix in large bowl; mix well. Add butter; stir with fork until mixture is crumbly.

3. Reserve 1 cup crumb mixture for topping. Press remaining crumb mixture onto bottom of prepared pan. Bake 7 to 8 minutes or until lightly browned.

4. Spread preserves over crust; sprinkle with reserved crumb mixture. Bake 23 to 25 minutes or until topping is golden brown. Cool completely in pan on wire rack.   *Makes 2 dozen bars*

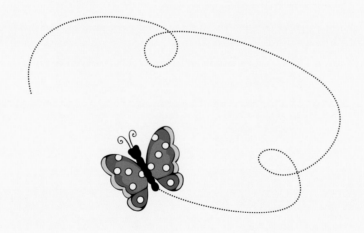

Fruit & Oat Squares

1 jar Fruit & Oat Squares Mix
⅔ cup butter, softened

1½ cups apricot, cherry or other
fruit flavor preserves

1. Preheat oven to 350°F. Lightly grease 13×9-inch baking pan.

2. Place bar cookie mix in large bowl; mix well. Add butter; stir with fork until mixture is crumbly.

3. Reserve 1 cup crumb mixture for topping. Press remaining crumb mixture onto bottom of prepared pan. Bake 7 to 8 minutes or until lightly browned.

4. Spread preserves over crust; sprinkle with reserved crumb mixture. Bake 23 to 25 minutes or until topping is golden brown. Cool completely in pan on wire rack.   *Makes 2 dozen bars*

Fruit & Oat Squares

1 jar Fruit & Oat Squares Mix
⅔ cup butter, softened

1½ cups apricot, cherry or other
fruit flavor preserves

1. Preheat oven to 350°F. Lightly grease 13×9-inch baking pan.

2. Place bar cookie mix in large bowl; mix well. Add butter; stir with fork until mixture is crumbly.

3. Reserve 1 cup crumb mixture for topping. Press remaining crumb mixture onto bottom of prepared pan. Bake 7 to 8 minutes or until lightly browned.

4. Spread preserves over crust; sprinkle with reserved crumb mixture. Bake 23 to 25 minutes or until topping is golden brown. Cool completely in pan on wire rack.   *Makes 2 dozen bars*

Fruit & Oat Squares

1 jar Fruit & Oat Squares Mix
⅔ cup butter, softened

1½ cups apricot, cherry or other
fruit flavor preserves

1. Preheat oven to 350°F. Lightly grease 13×9-inch baking pan.

2. Place bar cookie mix in large bowl; mix well. Add butter; stir with fork until mixture is crumbly.

3. Reserve 1 cup crumb mixture for topping. Press remaining crumb mixture onto bottom of prepared pan. Bake 7 to 8 minutes or until lightly browned.

4. Spread preserves over crust; sprinkle with reserved crumb mixture. Bake 23 to 25 minutes or until topping is golden brown. Cool completely in pan on wire rack.   *Makes 2 dozen bars*

Fruit & Oat Squares

1 jar Fruit & Oat Squares Mix
⅔ cup butter, softened

1½ cups apricot, cherry or other
fruit flavor preserves

1. Preheat oven to 350°F. Lightly grease 13×9-inch baking pan.

2. Place bar cookie mix in large bowl; mix well. Add butter; stir with fork until mixture is crumbly.

3. Reserve 1 cup crumb mixture for topping. Press remaining crumb mixture onto bottom of prepared pan. Bake 7 to 8 minutes or until lightly browned.

4. Spread preserves over crust; sprinkle with reserved crumb mixture. Bake 23 to 25 minutes or until topping is golden brown. Cool completely in pan on wire rack.

Makes 2 dozen bars

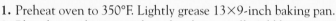

Fruit & Oat Squares

1 jar Fruit & Oat Squares Mix
⅔ cup butter, softened

1½ cups apricot, cherry or other
fruit flavor preserves

1. Preheat oven to 350°F. Lightly grease 13×9-inch baking pan.

2. Place bar cookie mix in large bowl; mix well. Add butter; stir with fork until mixture is crumbly.

3. Reserve 1 cup crumb mixture for topping. Press remaining crumb mixture onto bottom of prepared pan. Bake 7 to 8 minutes or until lightly browned.

4. Spread preserves over crust; sprinkle with reserved crumb mixture. Bake 23 to 25 minutes or until topping is golden brown. Cool completely in pan on wire rack.

Makes 2 dozen bars

Fruit & Oat Squares

1 jar Fruit & Oat Squares Mix
⅔ cup butter, softened

1½ cups apricot, cherry or other
fruit flavor preserves

1. Preheat oven to 350°F. Lightly grease 13×9-inch baking pan.

2. Place bar cookie mix in large bowl; mix well. Add butter; stir with fork until mixture is crumbly.

3. Reserve 1 cup crumb mixture for topping. Press remaining crumb mixture onto bottom of prepared pan. Bake 7 to 8 minutes or until lightly browned.

4. Spread preserves over crust; sprinkle with reserved crumb mixture. Bake 23 to 25 minutes or until topping is golden brown. Cool completely in pan on wire rack.

Makes 2 dozen bars

Chocolate-Coconut-Toffee Delights Mix

1 package (12 ounces) semisweet chocolate chips, divided
1½ cups flaked coconut
1 cup toffee baking pieces
¾ cup packed light brown sugar
½ cup all-purpose flour
¼ teaspoon baking powder
¼ teaspoon salt

1. Place 1 cup chocolate chips in resealable plastic food storage bag; seal bag. Layer all remaining ingredients attractively in any order into 1½-quart food storage jar with tight-fitting lid. Pack ingredients down slightly before adding another layer. Use chocolate chips in bag as final layer in jar.

2. Cover top of jar with fabric; attach gift tag with raffia or ribbon.

Makes one 1½-quart jar

Chocolate-Coconut-Toffee Delights

    1 jar Chocolate-Coconut-Toffee Delights Mix
    ¼ cup butter, cut into small pieces
    2 eggs
    1 teaspoon vanilla

1. Preheat oven to 350°F. Line cookie sheets with parchment paper. Place 1 cup chocolate chips from bag in large microwavable bowl. Microwave at HIGH 1 minute; stir. Microwave 30 to 60 seconds or until chips are melted; stir well.

2. Add butter to chocolate in bowl; stir until melted. Beat in eggs and vanilla until blended. Add remaining cookie mix to chocolate mixture; stir until blended.

3. Drop heaping ⅓ cupfuls dough 3 inches apart onto prepared cookie sheets. Flatten dough into 3½-inch rounds. Bake about 15 minutes or until edges are just firm to the touch. Let cookies stand on cookie sheets 2 minutes. Slide parchment paper and cookies onto countertop; cool.   *Makes 1 dozen (5-inch) cookies*

Chocolate-Coconut-Toffee Delights

1 jar Chocolate-Coconut-Toffee
Delights Mix
¼ cup butter, cut into pieces

2 eggs
1 teaspoon vanilla

1. Preheat oven to 350°F. Line cookie sheets with parchment paper. Place 1 cup chocolate chips from bag in large microwavable bowl. Microwave at HIGH 1 minute; stir. Microwave 30 to 60 seconds or until chips are melted; stir well. **2.** Add butter to chocolate in bowl; stir until melted. Beat in eggs and vanilla until blended. Add remaining cookie mix to chocolate mixture; stir until blended. **3.** Drop heaping ⅓ cupfuls dough 3 inches apart onto prepared cookie sheets. Flatten dough into 3½-inch rounds. Bake about 15 minutes or until edges are just firm to the touch. Let cookies stand on cookie sheets 2 minutes. Slide parchment paper and cookies onto countertop; cool. *Makes 1 dozen (5-inch) cookies*

Chocolate-Coconut-Toffee Delights

1 jar Chocolate-Coconut-Toffee
Delights Mix
¼ cup butter, cut into pieces

2 eggs
1 teaspoon vanilla

1. Preheat oven to 350°F. Line cookie sheets with parchment paper. Place 1 cup chocolate chips from bag in large microwavable bowl. Microwave at HIGH 1 minute; stir. Microwave 30 to 60 seconds or until chips are melted; stir well. **2.** Add butter to chocolate in bowl; stir until melted. Beat in eggs and vanilla until blended. Add remaining cookie mix to chocolate mixture; stir until blended. **3.** Drop heaping ⅓ cupfuls dough 3 inches apart onto prepared cookie sheets. Flatten dough into 3½-inch rounds. Bake about 15 minutes or until edges are just firm to the touch. Let cookies stand on cookie sheets 2 minutes. Slide parchment paper and cookies onto countertop; cool. *Makes 1 dozen (5-inch) cookies*

Chocolate-Coconut-Toffee Delights

1 jar Chocolate-Coconut-Toffee
Delights Mix
¼ cup butter, cut into pieces

2 eggs
1 teaspoon vanilla

1. Preheat oven to 350°F. Line cookie sheets with parchment paper. Place 1 cup chocolate chips from bag in large microwavable bowl. Microwave at HIGH 1 minute; stir. Microwave 30 to 60 seconds or until chips are melted; stir well. **2.** Add butter to chocolate in bowl; stir until melted. Beat in eggs and vanilla until blended. Add remaining cookie mix to chocolate mixture; stir until blended. **3.** Drop heaping ⅓ cupfuls dough 3 inches apart onto prepared cookie sheets. Flatten dough into 3½-inch rounds. Bake about 15 minutes or until edges are just firm to the touch. Let cookies stand on cookie sheets 2 minutes. Slide parchment paper and cookies onto countertop; cool. *Makes 1 dozen (5-inch) cookies*

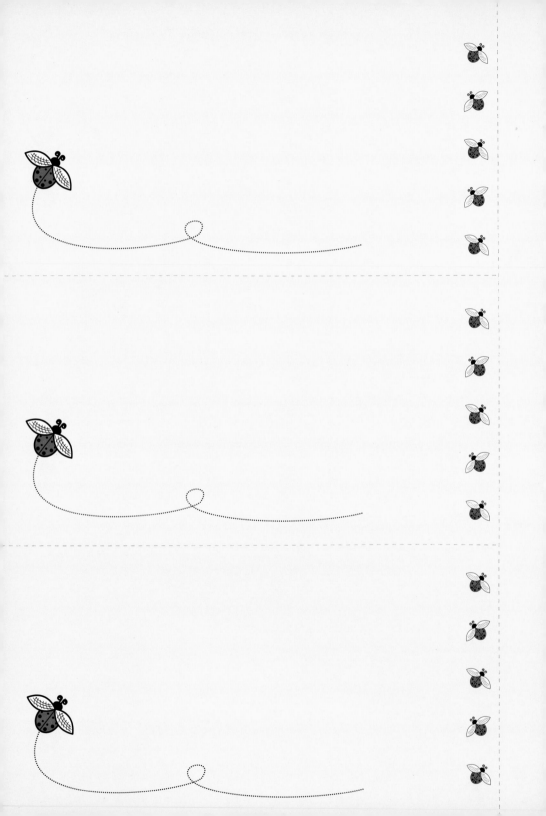

Chocolate-Coconut-Toffee Delights

1 jar Chocolate-Coconut-Toffee
   Delights Mix
¼ cup butter, cut into pieces

2 eggs
1 teaspoon vanilla

1. Preheat oven to 350°F. Line cookie sheets with parchment paper. Place 1 cup chocolate chips from bag in large microwavable bowl. Microwave at HIGH 1 minute; stir. Microwave 30 to 60 seconds or until chips are melted; stir well.
2. Add butter to chocolate in bowl; stir until melted. Beat in eggs and vanilla until blended. Add remaining cookie mix to chocolate mixture; stir until blended.
3. Drop heaping ⅓ cupfuls dough 3 inches apart onto prepared cookie sheets. Flatten dough into 3½-inch rounds. Bake about 15 minutes or until edges are just firm to the touch. Let cookies stand on cookie sheets 2 minutes. Slide parchment paper and cookies onto countertop; cool. *Makes 1 dozen (5-inch) cookies*

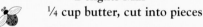

Chocolate-Coconut-Toffee Delights

1 jar Chocolate-Coconut-Toffee
   Delights Mix
¼ cup butter, cut into pieces

2 eggs
1 teaspoon vanilla

1. Preheat oven to 350°F. Line cookie sheets with parchment paper. Place 1 cup chocolate chips from bag in large microwavable bowl. Microwave at HIGH 1 minute; stir. Microwave 30 to 60 seconds or until chips are melted; stir well.
2. Add butter to chocolate in bowl; stir until melted. Beat in eggs and vanilla until blended. Add remaining cookie mix to chocolate mixture; stir until blended.
3. Drop heaping ⅓ cupfuls dough 3 inches apart onto prepared cookie sheets. Flatten dough into 3½-inch rounds. Bake about 15 minutes or until edges are just firm to the touch. Let cookies stand on cookie sheets 2 minutes. Slide parchment paper and cookies onto countertop; cool. *Makes 1 dozen (5-inch) cookies*

Chocolate-Coconut-Toffee Delights

1 jar Chocolate-Coconut-Toffee
   Delights Mix
¼ cup butter, cut into pieces

2 eggs
1 teaspoon vanilla

1. Preheat oven to 350°F. Line cookie sheets with parchment paper. Place 1 cup chocolate chips from bag in large microwavable bowl. Microwave at HIGH 1 minute; stir. Microwave 30 to 60 seconds or until chips are melted; stir well.

2. Add butter to chocolate in bowl; stir until melted. Beat in eggs and vanilla until blended. Add remaining cookie mix to chocolate mixture; stir until blended.
3. Drop heaping ⅓ cupfuls dough 3 inches apart onto prepared cookie sheets. Flatten dough into 3½-inch rounds. Bake about 15 minutes or until edges are just firm to the touch. Let cookies stand on cookie sheets 2 minutes. Slide parchment

paper and cookies onto countertop; cool. *Makes 1 dozen (5-inch) cookies*

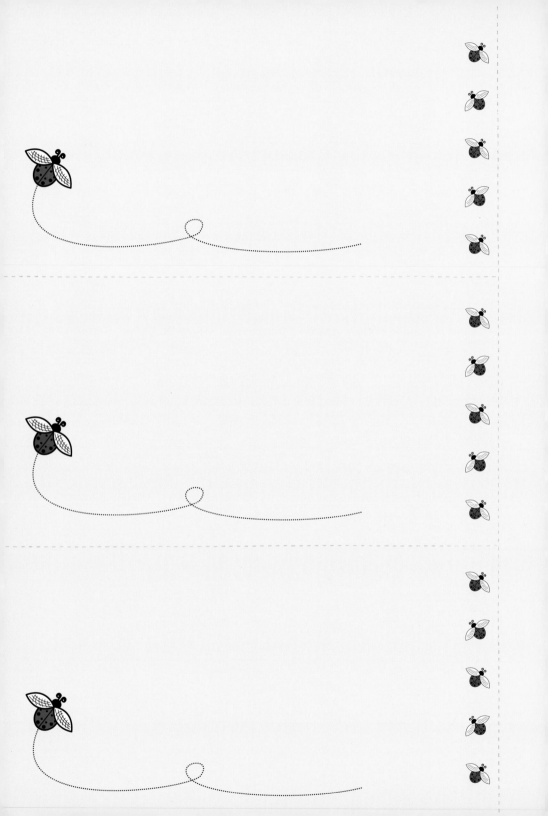

Linzer Bars Mix

3 cups all-purpose flour
1¾ cups whole almonds, ground
1 cup granulated sugar
1½ teaspoons grated lemon peel
1½ teaspoons ground cinnamon

1. Layer ingredients attractively in any order into 1½-quart food storage jar with tight-fitting lid. Pack ingredients down slightly before adding another layer.

2. Cover top of jar with fabric; attach gift tag with raffia or ribbon.

Makes one 1½-quart jar

Linzer Bars

1¾ cups butter, softened
1 egg
1 jar Linzer Bars Mix
¾ cup raspberry preserves
Powdered sugar

1. Preheat oven to 350°F. Lightly grease 13×9-inch baking pan.

2. Beat butter in large bowl until smooth. Add egg; beat until blended. (Mixture may appear curdled.) Add bar cookie mix to butter mixture; stir until well blended.

3. Press 3 cups dough into bottom of prepared pan. Spread preserves over crust. Press remaining dough, a small amount at a time, evenly over preserves.

4. Bake 40 to 45 minutes or until golden brown. Cool in pan on wire rack. Sprinkle with powdered sugar.   *Makes 2 dozen bars*

Linzer Bars

1¾ cups butter, softened ¾ cup raspberry preserves
1 egg Powdered sugar
1 jar Linzer Bars Mix

1. Preheat oven to 350°F. Lightly grease 13×9-inch baking pan.

2. Beat butter in large bowl until smooth. Add egg; beat until blended. (Mixture may appear curdled.) Add bar cookie mix to butter mixture; stir until well blended.

3. Press 3 cups dough into bottom of prepared pan. Spread preserves over crust. Press remaining dough, a small amount at a time, evenly over preserves.

4. Bake 40 to 45 minutes or until golden brown. Cool in pan on wire rack. Sprinkle with powdered sugar. *Makes 2 dozen bars*

Linzer Bars

1¾ cups butter, softened ¾ cup raspberry preserves
1 egg Powdered sugar
1 jar Linzer Bars Mix

1. Preheat oven to 350°F. Lightly grease 13×9-inch baking pan.

2. Beat butter in large bowl until smooth. Add egg; beat until blended. (Mixture may appear curdled.) Add bar cookie mix to butter mixture; stir until well blended.

3. Press 3 cups dough into bottom of prepared pan. Spread preserves over crust. Press remaining dough, a small amount at a time, evenly over preserves.

4. Bake 40 to 45 minutes or until golden brown. Cool in pan on wire rack. Sprinkle with powdered sugar. *Makes 2 dozen bars*

Linzer Bars

1¾ cups butter, softened ¾ cup raspberry preserves
1 egg Powdered sugar
1 jar Linzer Bars Mix

1. Preheat oven to 350°F. Lightly grease 13×9-inch baking pan.

2. Beat butter in large bowl until smooth. Add egg; beat until blended. (Mixture may appear curdled.) Add bar cookie mix to butter mixture; stir until well blended.

3. Press 3 cups dough into bottom of prepared pan. Spread preserves over crust. Press remaining dough, a small amount at a time, evenly over preserves.

4. Bake 40 to 45 minutes or until golden brown. Cool in pan on wire rack. Sprinkle with powdered sugar. *Makes 2 dozen bars*

Linzer Bars

1¾ cups butter, softened   ¾ cup raspberry preserves
1 egg   Powdered sugar

1 jar Linzer Bars Mix

1. Preheat oven to 350°F. Lightly grease 13×9-inch baking pan.
2. Beat butter in large bowl until smooth. Add egg; beat until blended. (Mixture may appear curdled.) Add bar cookie mix to butter mixture; stir until well blended.
3. Press 3 cups dough into bottom of prepared pan. Spread preserves over crust. Press remaining dough, a small amount at a time, evenly over preserves.
4. Bake 40 to 45 minutes or until golden brown. Cool in pan on wire rack. Sprinkle with powdered sugar.   *Makes 2 dozen bars*

Linzer Bars

1¾ cups butter, softened   ¾ cup raspberry preserves
1 egg   Powdered sugar
1 jar Linzer Bars Mix

1. Preheat oven to 350°F. Lightly grease 13×9-inch baking pan.
2. Beat butter in large bowl until smooth. Add egg; beat until blended. (Mixture may appear curdled.) Add bar cookie mix to butter mixture; stir until well blended.
3. Press 3 cups dough into bottom of prepared pan. Spread preserves over crust. Press remaining dough, a small amount at a time, evenly over preserves.
4. Bake 40 to 45 minutes or until golden brown. Cool in pan on wire rack. Sprinkle with powdered sugar.   *Makes 2 dozen bars*

Linzer Bars

1¾ cups butter, softened   ¾ cup raspberry preserves
1 egg   Powdered sugar
1 jar Linzer Bars Mix

1. Preheat oven to 350°F. Lightly grease 13×9-inch baking pan.
2. Beat butter in large bowl until smooth. Add egg; beat until blended. (Mixture may appear curdled.) Add bar cookie mix to butter mixture; stir until well blended.
3. Press 3 cups dough into bottom of prepared pan. Spread preserves over crust. Press remaining dough, a small amount at a time, evenly over preserves.
4. Bake 40 to 45 minutes or until golden brown. Cool in pan on wire rack. Sprinkle with powdered sugar.   *Makes 2 dozen bars*

Oatmeal Candied Chippers Mix

2¾ cups uncooked old-fashioned or quick oats
¾ cup granulated sugar
¾ cup all-purpose flour
¾ cup packed light brown sugar
¾ cup candy-coated semisweet chocolate chips or candy-coated
    chocolate pieces
¾ teaspoon salt
½ teaspoon baking soda

1. Layer ingredients attractively in any order into 1½-quart food storage jar with tight-fitting lid. Pack ingredients down slightly before adding another layer.

2. Cover top of jar with fabric; attach gift tag with raffia or ribbon.

Makes one 1½-quart jar

Oatmeal Candied Chippers

¾ cup butter, softened
3 tablespoons milk
1 egg
2 teaspoons vanilla
1 jar Oatmeal Candied Chippers Mix

1. Preheat oven to 375°F. Lightly grease cookie sheets.

2. Beat butter in large bowl until smooth. Beat in milk, egg and vanilla until blended. (Mixture may appear curdled.) Add cookie mix to butter mixture; stir until well blended.

3. Drop rounded tablespoonfuls dough 2 inches apart onto prepared cookie sheets. Bake 10 to 12 minutes or until edges are golden brown. Let cookies stand on cookie sheets 2 minutes. Remove cookies to wire racks to cool completely.

Makes about 4 dozen cookies

Oatmeal Candied Chippers

¾ cup butter, softened   2 teaspoons vanilla
3 tablespoons milk   1 jar Oatmeal Candied
1 egg   Chippers Mix

1. Preheat oven to 375°F. Lightly grease cookie sheets.
2. Beat butter in large bowl until smooth. Beat in milk, egg and vanilla until blended. (Mixture may appear curdled.) Add cookie mix to butter mixture; stir until well blended.
3. Drop rounded tablespoonfuls dough 2 inches apart onto prepared cookie sheets. Bake 10 to 12 minutes or until edges are golden brown. Let cookies stand on cookie sheets 2 minutes. Remove cookies to wire racks to cool completely.

Makes about 4 dozen cookies

Oatmeal Candied Chippers

¾ cup butter, softened   2 teaspoons vanilla
3 tablespoons milk   1 jar Oatmeal Candied
1 egg   Chippers Mix

1. Preheat oven to 375°F. Lightly grease cookie sheets.
2. Beat butter in large bowl until smooth. Beat in milk, egg and vanilla until blended. (Mixture may appear curdled.) Add cookie mix to butter mixture; stir until well blended.
3. Drop rounded tablespoonfuls dough 2 inches apart onto prepared cookie sheets. Bake 10 to 12 minutes or until edges are golden brown. Let cookies stand on cookie sheets 2 minutes. Remove cookies to wire racks to cool completely.

Makes about 4 dozen cookies

Oatmeal Candied Chippers

¾ cup butter, softened   2 teaspoons vanilla
3 tablespoons milk   1 jar Oatmeal Candied
1 egg   Chippers Mix

1. Preheat oven to 375°F. Lightly grease cookie sheets.
2. Beat butter in large bowl until smooth. Beat in milk, egg and vanilla until blended. (Mixture may appear curdled.) Add cookie mix to butter mixture; stir until well blended.
3. Drop rounded tablespoonfuls dough 2 inches apart onto prepared cookie sheets. Bake 10 to 12 minutes or until edges are golden brown. Let cookies stand on cookie sheets 2 minutes. Remove cookies to wire racks to cool completely.

Makes about 4 dozen cookies

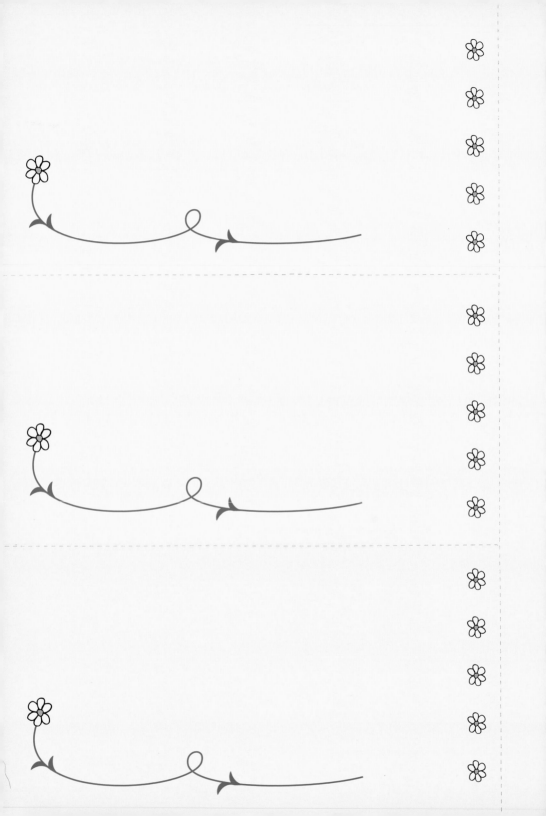

Oatmeal Candied Chippers

¾ cup butter, softened
3 tablespoons milk
1 egg

2 teaspoons vanilla
1 jar Oatmeal Candied
Chippers Mix

1. Preheat oven to 375°F. Lightly grease cookie sheets.

2. Beat butter in large bowl until smooth. Beat in milk, egg and vanilla until blended. (Mixture may appear curdled.) Add cookie mix to butter mixture; stir until well blended.

3. Drop rounded tablespoonfuls dough 2 inches apart onto prepared cookie sheets. Bake 10 to 12 minutes or until edges are golden brown. Let cookies stand on cookie sheets 2 minutes. Remove cookies to wire racks to cool completely.

Makes about 4 dozen cookies

Oatmeal Candied Chippers

¾ cup butter, softened
3 tablespoons milk
1 egg

2 teaspoons vanilla
1 jar Oatmeal Candied
Chippers Mix

1. Preheat oven to 375°F. Lightly grease cookie sheets.

2. Beat butter in large bowl until smooth. Beat in milk, egg and vanilla until blended. (Mixture may appear curdled.) Add cookie mix to butter mixture; stir until well blended.

3. Drop rounded tablespoonfuls dough 2 inches apart onto prepared cookie sheets. Bake 10 to 12 minutes or until edges are golden brown. Let cookies stand on cookie sheets 2 minutes. Remove cookies to wire racks to cool completely.

Makes about 4 dozen cookies

Oatmeal Candied Chippers

¾ cup butter, softened
3 tablespoons milk
1 egg

2 teaspoons vanilla
1 jar Oatmeal Candied
Chippers Mix

1. Preheat oven to 375°F. Lightly grease cookie sheets.

2. Beat butter in large bowl until smooth. Beat in milk, egg and vanilla until blended. (Mixture may appear curdled.) Add cookie mix to butter mixture; stir until well blended.

3. Drop rounded tablespoonfuls dough 2 inches apart onto prepared cookie sheets. Bake 10 to 12 minutes or until edges are golden brown. Let cookies stand on cookie sheets 2 minutes. Remove cookies to wire racks to cool completely.

Makes about 4 dozen cookies

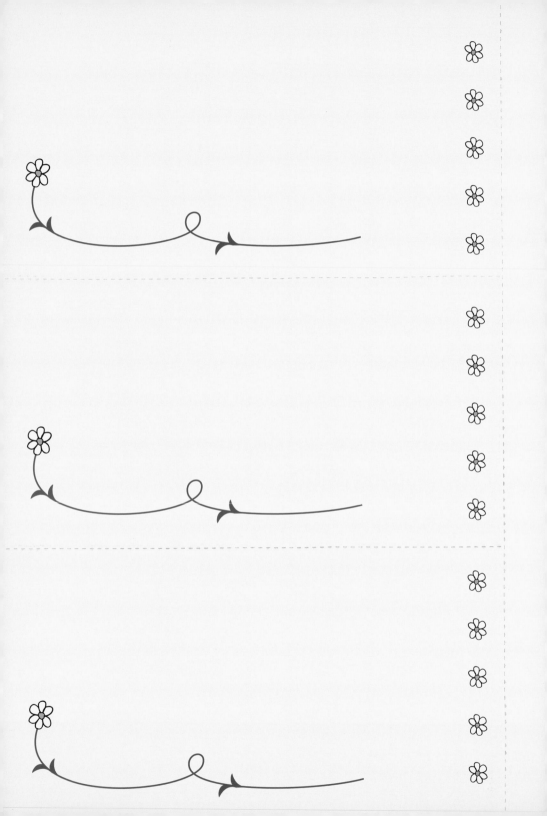

Rocky Road Brownies Mix

   1 cup sugar
   1 cup semisweet chocolate chips
   ¾ cup coarsely chopped walnuts
   ½ cup all-purpose flour
   ½ cup unsweetened cocoa powder
   1 cup miniature marshmallows

1. Layer all ingredients except marshmallows attractively in any order into 1-quart food storage jar with tight-fitting lid. Pack ingredients down slightly before adding another layer. Place marshmallows in resealable plastic food storage bag; seal bag. Use marshmallows as final layer in jar.

2. Cover top of jar with fabric; attach gift tag with raffia or ribbon.

Makes one 1-quart jar

Rocky Road Brownies

1 jar Rocky Road Brownies Mix
½ cup butter, melted
¼ cup buttermilk
1 egg
1 teaspoon vanilla

1. Preheat oven to 350°F. Lightly grease 8×8-inch baking pan. Remove marshmallows from plastic food storage bag in jar; set aside.

2. Place remaining brownie mix in large bowl. Add melted butter, buttermilk, egg and vanilla; stir until well blended.

3. Spread batter evenly in prepared pan. Bake 25 to 30 minutes or until set. Sprinkle with reserved marshmallows. Bake 3 to 5 minutes or until marshmallows are puffed and slightly melted. Cool in pan on wire rack. *Makes 16 brownies*

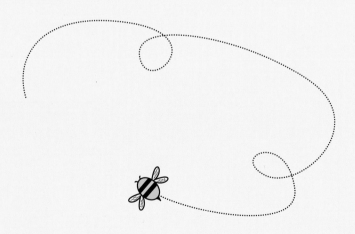

Rocky Road Brownies

1 jar Rocky Road Brownies
Mix
½ cup butter, melted

¼ cup buttermilk
1 egg
1 teaspoon vanilla

1. Preheat oven to 350°F. Lightly grease 8×8-inch baking pan. Remove marshmallows from plastic food storage bag in jar; set aside.

2. Place remaining brownie mix in large bowl. Add melted butter, buttermilk, egg and vanilla; stir until well blended.

3. Spread batter evenly in prepared pan. Bake 25 to 30 minutes or until set. Sprinkle with reserved marshmallows. Bake 3 to 5 minutes or until marshmallows are puffed and slightly melted. Cool in pan on wire rack.   *Makes 16 brownies*

Rocky Road Brownies

1 jar Rocky Road Brownies
Mix
½ cup butter, melted

¼ cup buttermilk
1 egg
1 teaspoon vanilla

1. Preheat oven to 350°F. Lightly grease 8×8-inch baking pan. Remove marshmallows from plastic food storage bag in jar; set aside.

2. Place remaining brownie mix in large bowl. Add melted butter, buttermilk, egg and vanilla; stir until well blended.

3. Spread batter evenly in prepared pan. Bake 25 to 30 minutes or until set. Sprinkle with reserved marshmallows. Bake 3 to 5 minutes or until marshmallows are puffed and slightly melted. Cool in pan on wire rack.   *Makes 16 brownies*

Rocky Road Brownies

1 jar Rocky Road Brownies
Mix
½ cup butter, melted

¼ cup buttermilk
1 egg
1 teaspoon vanilla

1. Preheat oven to 350°F. Lightly grease 8×8-inch baking pan. Remove marshmallows from plastic food storage bag in jar; set aside.

2. Place remaining brownie mix in large bowl. Add melted butter, buttermilk, egg and vanilla; stir until well blended.

3. Spread batter evenly in prepared pan. Bake 25 to 30 minutes or until set. Sprinkle with reserved marshmallows. Bake 3 to 5 minutes or until marshmallows are puffed and slightly melted. Cool in pan on wire rack.   *Makes 16 brownies*

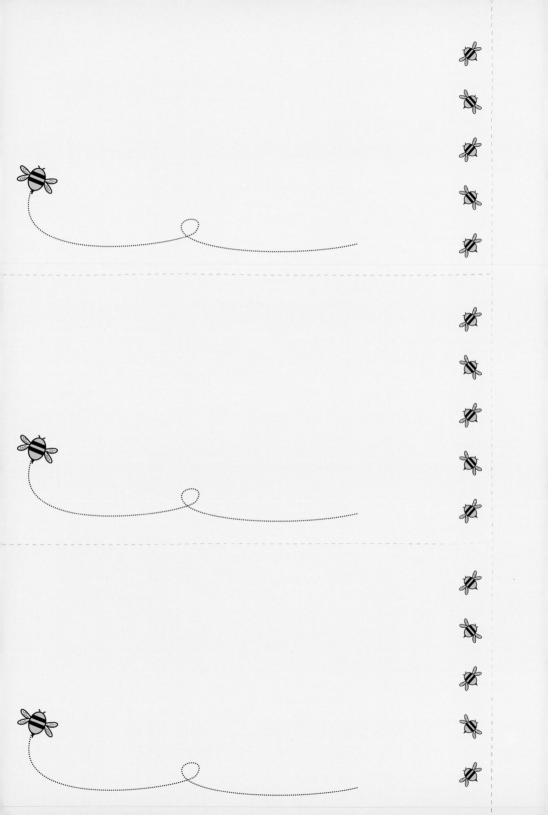

Rocky Road Brownies

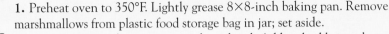

1 jar Rocky Road Brownies Mix	¼ cup buttermilk
	1 egg
½ cup butter, melted	1 teaspoon vanilla

1. Preheat oven to 350°F. Lightly grease 8×8-inch baking pan. Remove marshmallows from plastic food storage bag in jar; set aside.

2. Place remaining brownie mix in large bowl. Add melted butter, buttermilk, egg and vanilla; stir until well blended.

3. Spread batter evenly in prepared pan. Bake 25 to 30 minutes or until set. Sprinkle with reserved marshmallows. Bake 3 to 5 minutes or until marshmallows are puffed and slightly melted. Cool in pan on wire rack.   *Makes 16 brownies*

Rocky Road Brownies

1 jar Rocky Road Brownies Mix	¼ cup buttermilk
	1 egg
½ cup butter, melted	1 teaspoon vanilla

1. Preheat oven to 350°F. Lightly grease 8×8-inch baking pan. Remove marshmallows from plastic food storage bag in jar; set aside.

2. Place remaining brownie mix in large bowl. Add melted butter, buttermilk, egg and vanilla; stir until well blended.

3. Spread batter evenly in prepared pan. Bake 25 to 30 minutes or until set. Sprinkle with reserved marshmallows. Bake 3 to 5 minutes or until marshmallows are puffed and slightly melted. Cool in pan on wire rack.   *Makes 16 brownies*

Rocky Road Brownies

1 jar Rocky Road Brownies Mix	¼ cup buttermilk
	1 egg
½ cup butter, melted	1 teaspoon vanilla

1. Preheat oven to 350°F. Lightly grease 8×8-inch baking pan. Remove marshmallows from plastic food storage bag in jar; set aside.

2. Place remaining brownie mix in large bowl. Add melted butter, buttermilk, egg and vanilla; stir until well blended.

3. Spread batter evenly in prepared pan. Bake 25 to 30 minutes or until set. Sprinkle with reserved marshmallows. Bake 3 to 5 minutes or until marshmallows are puffed and slightly melted. Cool in pan on wire rack.   *Makes 16 brownies*

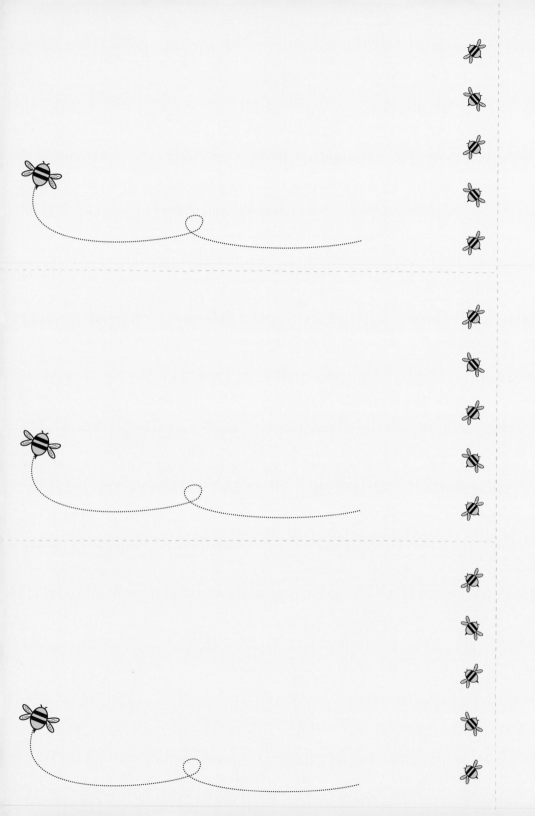

Orange Walnut Chip Cookies Mix

1½ cups uncooked old-fashioned oats
1 cup packed light brown sugar
1 cup semisweet chocolate chips
½ cup all-purpose flour
½ cup coarsely chopped walnuts
1 tablespoon grated orange peel
¼ teaspoon salt
¼ teaspoon baking soda

1. Layer ingredients attractively in any order into 1-quart food storage jar with tight-fitting lid. Pack ingredients down slightly before adding another layer.

2. Cover top of jar with fabric; attach gift tag with raffia or ribbon.

Makes one 1-quart jar

Orange Walnut Chip Cookies

½ cup butter, softened
1 egg
1 jar Orange Walnut Chip Cookies Mix

1. Preheat oven to 375°F. Lightly grease cookie sheets.

2. Beat butter in large bowl until smooth. Beat in egg until blended. (Mixture may appear curdled.) Add cookie mix to butter mixture; stir until well blended.

3. Drop rounded teaspoonfuls dough 2 inches apart onto prepared cookie sheets. Bake 8 to 10 minutes or until edges are golden brown. Let cookies stand on cookie sheets 2 minutes. Remove cookies to wire racks to cool completely.

Makes 3½ dozen cookies

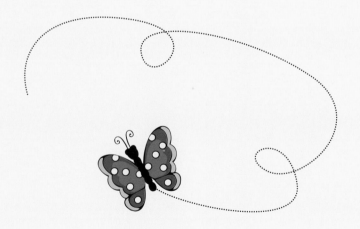

Orange Walnut Chip Cookies

½ cup butter, softened
1 egg

1 jar Orange Walnut Chip
Cookies Mix

1. Preheat oven to 375°F. Lightly grease cookie sheets.
2. Beat butter in large bowl until smooth. Beat in egg until blended. (Mixture may appear curdled.) Add cookie mix to butter mixture; stir until well blended.
3. Drop rounded teaspoonfuls dough 2 inches apart onto prepared cookie sheets. Bake 8 to 10 minutes or until edges are golden brown. Let cookies stand on cookie sheets 2 minutes. Remove cookies to wire racks to cool completely.

Makes 3½ dozen cookies

Orange Walnut Chip Cookies

½ cup butter, softened
1 egg

1 jar Orange Walnut Chip
Cookies Mix

1. Preheat oven to 375°F. Lightly grease cookie sheets.
2. Beat butter in large bowl until smooth. Beat in egg until blended. (Mixture may appear curdled.) Add cookie mix to butter mixture; stir until well blended.
3. Drop rounded teaspoonfuls dough 2 inches apart onto prepared cookie sheets. Bake 8 to 10 minutes or until edges are golden brown. Let cookies stand on cookie sheets 2 minutes. Remove cookies to wire racks to cool completely.

Makes 3½ dozen cookies

Orange Walnut Chip Cookies

½ cup butter, softened
1 egg

1 jar Orange Walnut Chip
Cookies Mix

1. Preheat oven to 375°F. Lightly grease cookie sheets.
2. Beat butter in large bowl until smooth. Beat in egg until blended. (Mixture may appear curdled.) Add cookie mix to butter mixture; stir until well blended.
3. Drop rounded teaspoonfuls dough 2 inches apart onto prepared cookie sheets. Bake 8 to 10 minutes or until edges are golden brown. Let cookies stand on cookie sheets 2 minutes. Remove cookies to wire racks to cool completely.

Makes 3½ dozen cookies

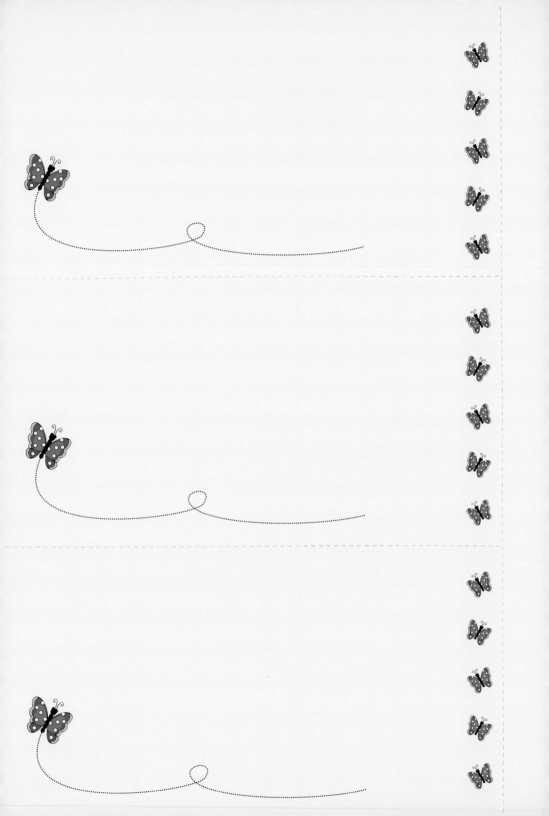

Orange Walnut Chip Cookies

½ cup butter, softened   1 jar Orange Walnut Chip
1 egg   Cookies Mix

1. Preheat oven to 375°F. Lightly grease cookie sheets.
2. Beat butter in large bowl until smooth. Beat in egg until blended. (Mixture may appear curdled.) Add cookie mix to butter mixture; stir until well blended.
3. Drop rounded teaspoonfuls dough 2 inches apart onto prepared cookie sheets. Bake 8 to 10 minutes or until edges are golden brown. Let cookies stand on cookie sheets 2 minutes. Remove cookies to wire racks to cool completely.

Makes 3½ dozen cookies

Orange Walnut Chip Cookies

½ cup butter, softened   1 jar Orange Walnut Chip
1 egg   Cookies Mix

1. Preheat oven to 375°F. Lightly grease cookie sheets.
2. Beat butter in large bowl until smooth. Beat in egg until blended. (Mixture may appear curdled.) Add cookie mix to butter mixture; stir until well blended.
3. Drop rounded teaspoonfuls dough 2 inches apart onto prepared cookie sheets. Bake 8 to 10 minutes or until edges are golden brown. Let cookies stand on cookie sheets 2 minutes. Remove cookies to wire racks to cool completely.

Makes 3½ dozen cookies

Orange Walnut Chip Cookies

½ cup butter, softened   1 jar Orange Walnut Chip
1 egg   Cookies Mix

1. Preheat oven to 375°F. Lightly grease cookie sheets.
2. Beat butter in large bowl until smooth. Beat in egg until blended. (Mixture may appear curdled.) Add cookie mix to butter mixture; stir until well blended.
3. Drop rounded teaspoonfuls dough 2 inches apart onto prepared cookie sheets. Bake 8 to 10 minutes or until edges are golden brown. Let cookies stand on cookie sheets 2 minutes. Remove cookies to wire racks to cool completely.

Makes 3½ dozen cookies

Strawberry Oat Bars Mix

2¼ cups uncooked quick oats
1 cup all-purpose flour
1 cup packed light brown sugar
2 teaspoons baking soda
½ teaspoon ground cinnamon
¼ teaspoon salt

1. Layer ingredients attractively in any order into 1-quart food storage jar with tight-fitting lid. Pack ingredients down slightly before adding another layer.

2. Cover top of jar with fabric; attach gift tag with raffia or ribbon.

Makes one 1-quart jar

Strawberry Oat Bars

1 cup butter, softened
1 jar Strawberry Oat Bars Mix
1 can (21 ounces) strawberry pie filling
¾ teaspoon almond extract

1. Preheat oven to 375°F.

2. Beat butter in large bowl until smooth. Add bar cookie mix to butter; beat until well blended and crumbly.

3. Press ⅔ of crumb mixture onto bottom of ungreased 13×9-inch baking pan. Bake 15 minutes; let cool 5 minutes on wire rack.

4. Place pie filling in food processor; process until smooth. Stir in almond extract.

5. Pour filling mixture over crust. Sprinkle remaining crumb mixture evenly over filling. Return pan to oven; bake 20 to 25 minutes or until topping is golden and filling is slightly bubbly. Cool completely on wire rack.   *Makes 2½ dozen bars*

Strawberry Oat Bars

1 cup butter, softened
1 jar Strawberry Oat Bars
   Mix

1 can (21 ounces) strawberry
   pie filling
¾ teaspoon almond extract

1. Preheat oven to 375°F.

2. Beat butter in large bowl until smooth. Add bar cookie mix to butter; beat until well blended and crumbly.

3. Press ⅔ of crumb mixture onto bottom of ungreased 13×9-inch baking pan. Bake 15 minutes; let cool 5 minutes on wire rack.

4. Place pie filling in food processor; process until smooth. Stir in almond extract.

5. Pour filling mixture over crust. Sprinkle remaining crumb mixture evenly over filling. Return pan to oven; bake 20 to 25 minutes or until topping is golden and filling is slightly bubbly. Cool completely on wire rack.   *Makes 2½ dozen bars*

Strawberry Oat Bars

1 cup butter, softened
1 jar Strawberry Oat Bars
   Mix

1 can (21 ounces) strawberry
   pie filling
¾ teaspoon almond extract

1. Preheat oven to 375°F.

2. Beat butter in large bowl until smooth. Add bar cookie mix to butter; beat until well blended and crumbly.

3. Press ⅔ of crumb mixture onto bottom of ungreased 13×9-inch baking pan. Bake 15 minutes; let cool 5 minutes on wire rack.

4. Place pie filling in food processor; process until smooth. Stir in almond extract.

5. Pour filling mixture over crust. Sprinkle remaining crumb mixture evenly over filling. Return pan to oven; bake 20 to 25 minutes or until topping is golden and filling is slightly bubbly. Cool completely on wire rack.   *Makes 2½ dozen bars*

Strawberry Oat Bars

1 cup butter, softened
1 jar Strawberry Oat Bars
   Mix

1 can (21 ounces) strawberry
   pie filling
¾ teaspoon almond extract

1. Preheat oven to 375°F.

2. Beat butter in large bowl until smooth. Add bar cookie mix to butter; beat until well blended and crumbly.

3. Press ⅔ of crumb mixture onto bottom of ungreased 13×9-inch baking pan. Bake 15 minutes; let cool 5 minutes on wire rack.

4. Place pie filling in food processor; process until smooth. Stir in almond extract.

5. Pour filling mixture over crust. Sprinkle remaining crumb mixture evenly over filling. Return pan to oven; bake 20 to 25 minutes or until topping is golden and filling is slightly bubbly. Cool completely on wire rack.   *Makes 2½ dozen bars*

Strawberry Oat Bars

1 cup butter, softened
1 jar Strawberry Oat Bars
 Mix

1 can (21 ounces) strawberry
 pie filling
¾ teaspoon almond extract

1. Preheat oven to 375°F.

2. Beat butter in large bowl until smooth. Add bar cookie mix to butter; beat until well blended and crumbly.

3. Press ⅔ of crumb mixture onto bottom of ungreased 13×9-inch baking pan. Bake 15 minutes; let cool 5 minutes on wire rack.

4. Place pie filling in food processor; process until smooth. Stir in almond extract.

5. Pour filling mixture over crust. Sprinkle remaining crumb mixture evenly over filling. Return pan to oven; bake 20 to 25 minutes or until topping is golden and filling is slightly bubbly. Cool completely on wire rack.   *Makes 2½ dozen bars*

Strawberry Oat Bars

1 cup butter, softened
1 jar Strawberry Oat Bars
 Mix

1 can (21 ounces) strawberry
 pie filling
¾ teaspoon almond extract

1. Preheat oven to 375°F.

2. Beat butter in large bowl until smooth. Add bar cookie mix to butter; beat until well blended and crumbly.

3. Press ⅔ of crumb mixture onto bottom of ungreased 13×9-inch baking pan. Bake 15 minutes; let cool 5 minutes on wire rack.

4. Place pie filling in food processor; process until smooth. Stir in almond extract.

5. Pour filling mixture over crust. Sprinkle remaining crumb mixture evenly over filling. Return pan to oven; bake 20 to 25 minutes or until topping is golden and filling is slightly bubbly. Cool completely on wire rack.   *Makes 2½ dozen bars*

Strawberry Oat Bars

1 cup butter, softened
1 jar Strawberry Oat Bars
 Mix

1 can (21 ounces) strawberry
 pie filling
¾ teaspoon almond extract

1. Preheat oven to 375°F.

2. Beat butter in large bowl until smooth. Add bar cookie mix to butter; beat until well blended and crumbly.

3. Press ⅔ of crumb mixture onto bottom of ungreased 13×9-inch baking pan. Bake 15 minutes; let cool 5 minutes on wire rack.

4. Place pie filling in food processor; process until smooth. Stir in almond extract.

5. Pour filling mixture over crust. Sprinkle remaining crumb mixture evenly over filling. Return pan to oven; bake 20 to 25 minutes or until topping is golden and filling is slightly bubbly. Cool completely on wire rack.   *Makes 2½ dozen bars*

Super Chocolate Cookies Mix

1½ cups all-purpose flour
  1 cup packed light brown sugar
  ¾ cup candy-coated chocolate pieces
  ½ cup salted peanuts, coarsely chopped
  ½ cup raisins
  ¼ cup unsweetened cocoa powder
  ¾ teaspoon baking soda
  ¼ teaspoon salt

1. Layer ingredients attractively in any order into 1-quart food storage jar with tight-fitting lid. Pack ingredients down slightly before adding another layer.

2. Cover top of jar with fabric; attach gift tag with raffia or ribbon.

Makes one 1-quart jar

69

Super Chocolate Cookies

⅔ cup butter, softened
2 eggs
1½ teaspoons vanilla
1 jar Super Chocolate Cookies Mix

1. Preheat oven to 350°F.

2. Beat butter in large bowl until smooth. Beat in eggs and vanilla until blended. (Mixture may appear curdled.) Add cookie mix to butter mixture; stir until well blended.

3. Drop heaping tablespoonfuls dough 2 inches apart onto ungreased cookie sheets. Bake 11 to 12 minutes or until almost set. Let cookies stand on cookie sheets 2 minutes. Remove cookies to wire racks to cool completely. *Makes 2 dozen cookies*

Super Chocolate Cookies

⅔ cup butter, softened
2 eggs
1½ teaspoons vanilla

1 jar Super Chocolate Cookies Mix

1. Preheat oven to 350°F.

2. Beat butter in large bowl until smooth. Beat in eggs and vanilla until blended. (Mixture may appear curdled.) Add cookie mix to butter mixture; stir until well blended.

3. Drop heaping tablespoonfuls dough 2 inches apart onto ungreased cookie sheets. Bake 11 to 12 minutes or until almost set. Let cookies stand on cookie sheets 2 minutes. Remove cookies to wire racks to cool completely.

Makes 2 dozen cookies

Super Chocolate Cookies

⅔ cup butter, softened
2 eggs
1½ teaspoons vanilla

1 jar Super Chocolate Cookies Mix

1. Preheat oven to 350°F.

2. Beat butter in large bowl until smooth. Beat in eggs and vanilla until blended. (Mixture may appear curdled.) Add cookie mix to butter mixture; stir until well blended.

3. Drop heaping tablespoonfuls dough 2 inches apart onto ungreased cookie sheets. Bake 11 to 12 minutes or until almost set. Let cookies stand on cookie sheets 2 minutes. Remove cookies to wire racks to cool completely.

Makes 2 dozen cookies

Super Chocolate Cookies

⅔ cup butter, softened
2 eggs
1½ teaspoons vanilla

1 jar Super Chocolate Cookies Mix

1. Preheat oven to 350°F.

2. Beat butter in large bowl until smooth. Beat in eggs and vanilla until blended. (Mixture may appear curdled.) Add cookie mix to butter mixture; stir until well blended.

3. Drop heaping tablespoonfuls dough 2 inches apart onto ungreased cookie sheets. Bake 11 to 12 minutes or until almost set. Let cookies stand on cookie sheets 2 minutes. Remove cookies to wire racks to cool completely.

Makes 2 dozen cookies

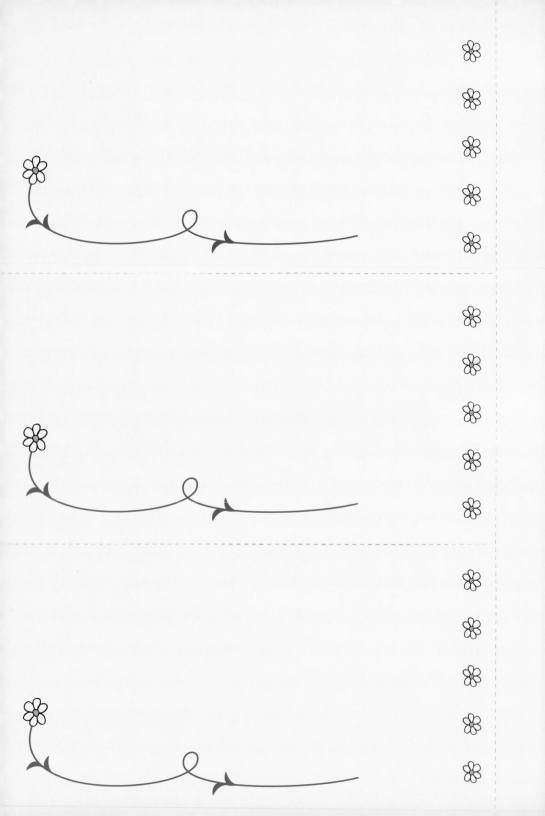

Super Chocolate Cookies

⅔ cup butter, softened
2 eggs
1½ teaspoons vanilla

1 jar Super Chocolate Cookies Mix

1. Preheat oven to 350°F.

2. Beat butter in large bowl until smooth. Beat in eggs and vanilla until blended. (Mixture may appear curdled.) Add cookie mix to butter mixture; stir until well blended.

3. Drop heaping tablespoonfuls dough 2 inches apart onto ungreased cookie sheets. Bake 11 to 12 minutes or until almost set. Let cookies stand on cookie sheets 2 minutes. Remove cookies to wire racks to cool completely.

Makes 2 dozen cookies

Super Chocolate Cookies

⅔ cup butter, softened
2 eggs
1½ teaspoons vanilla

1 jar Super Chocolate Cookies Mix

1. Preheat oven to 350°F.

2. Beat butter in large bowl until smooth. Beat in eggs and vanilla until blended. (Mixture may appear curdled.) Add cookie mix to butter mixture; stir until well blended.

3. Drop heaping tablespoonfuls dough 2 inches apart onto ungreased cookie sheets. Bake 11 to 12 minutes or until almost set. Let cookies stand on cookie sheets 2 minutes. Remove cookies to wire racks to cool completely.

Makes 2 dozen cookies

Super Chocolate Cookies

⅔ cup butter, softened
2 eggs
1½ teaspoons vanilla

1 jar Super Chocolate Cookies Mix

1. Preheat oven to 350°F.

2. Beat butter in large bowl until smooth. Beat in eggs and vanilla until blended. (Mixture may appear curdled.) Add cookie mix to butter mixture; stir until well blended.

3. Drop heaping tablespoonfuls dough 2 inches apart onto ungreased cookie sheets. Bake 11 to 12 minutes or until almost set. Let cookies stand on cookie sheets 2 minutes. Remove cookies to wire racks to cool completely.

Makes 2 dozen cookies

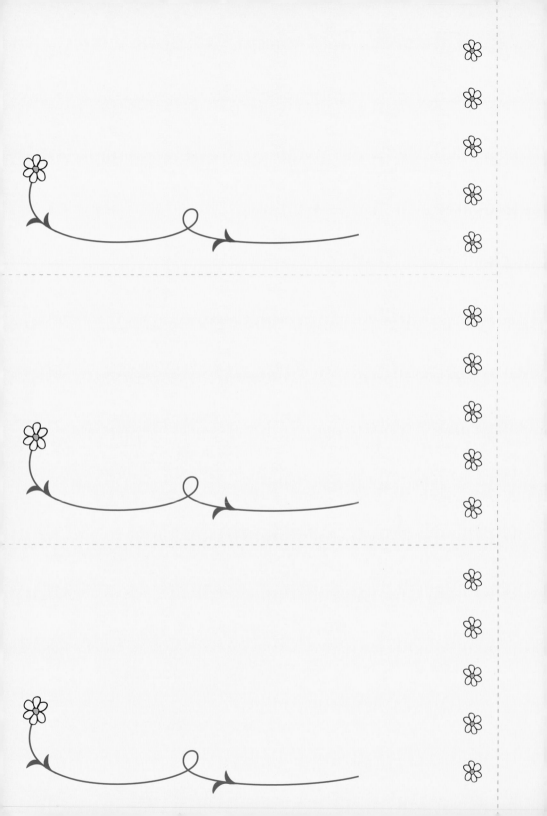

White Chocolate Chunk Muffin Mix

2½ cups all-purpose flour

1½ cups chopped white chocolate chunks or chips

1 cup packed brown sugar

⅓ cup unsweetened cocoa powder

2 teaspoons baking soda

½ teaspoon salt

1. Layer ingredients attractively in any order into 1-quart food storage jar with tight-fitting lid. Pack ingredients down slightly before adding another layer.

2. Cover top of jar with fabric; attach gift tag with raffia or ribbon.

Makes one 1-quart jar

White Chocolate Chunk Muffins

1 jar White Chocolate Chunk Muffin Mix
1⅓ cups buttermilk
6 tablespoons butter, melted
2 eggs, beaten
1½ teaspoons vanilla

1. Preheat oven to 400°F. Grease or paper-line 18 regular-size (2½-inch) muffin cups.

2. Pour contents of jar into large bowl. Combine buttermilk, butter, eggs and vanilla in small bowl until blended; stir into jar mixture just until moistened. Spoon evenly into prepared muffin cups, filling about ⅔ full.

3. Bake 16 to 18 minutes or until toothpick inserted in centers comes out clean. Cool in pans on wire racks 5 minutes; remove from pans and cool 10 minutes on wire racks.   *Makes 18 muffins*

White Chocolate Chunk Muffins

1 jar White Chocolate Chunk
Muffin Mix
1⅓ cups buttermilk

6 tablespoons butter, melted
2 eggs, beaten
1½ teaspoons vanilla

1. Preheat oven to 400°F. Grease or paper-line 18 regular-size (2½-inch) muffin cups.

2. Pour contents of jar into large bowl. Combine buttermilk, butter, eggs and vanilla in small bowl until blended; stir into jar mixture just until moistened. Spoon evenly into prepared muffin cups, filling about ⅔ full.

3. Bake 16 to 18 minutes or until toothpick inserted in centers comes out clean. Cool in pans on wire racks 5 minutes; remove from pans and cool 10 minutes on wire racks.

Makes 18 muffins

White Chocolate Chunk Muffins

1 jar White Chocolate Chunk
Muffin Mix
1⅓ cups buttermilk

6 tablespoons butter, melted
2 eggs, beaten
1½ teaspoons vanilla

1. Preheat oven to 400°F. Grease or paper-line 18 regular-size (2½-inch) muffin cups.

2. Pour contents of jar into large bowl. Combine buttermilk, butter, eggs and vanilla in small bowl until blended; stir into jar mixture just until moistened. Spoon evenly into prepared muffin cups, filling about ⅔ full.

3. Bake 16 to 18 minutes or until toothpick inserted in centers comes out clean. Cool in pans on wire racks 5 minutes; remove from pans and cool 10 minutes on wire racks.

Makes 18 muffins

White Chocolate Chunk Muffins

1 jar White Chocolate Chunk
Muffin Mix
1⅓ cups buttermilk

6 tablespoons butter, melted
2 eggs, beaten
1½ teaspoons vanilla

1. Preheat oven to 400°F. Grease or paper-line 18 regular-size (2½-inch) muffin cups.

2. Pour contents of jar into large bowl. Combine buttermilk, butter, eggs and vanilla in small bowl until blended; stir into jar mixture just until moistened. Spoon evenly into prepared muffin cups, filling about ⅔ full.

3. Bake 16 to 18 minutes or until toothpick inserted in centers comes out clean. Cool in pans on wire racks 5 minutes; remove from pans and cool 10 minutes on wire racks.

Makes 18 muffins

White Chocolate Chunk Muffins

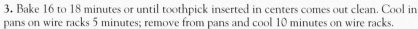

1 jar White Chocolate Chunk
Muffin Mix
1⅓ cups buttermilk

6 tablespoons butter, melted
2 eggs, beaten
1½ teaspoons vanilla

1. Preheat oven to 400°F. Grease or paper-line 18 regular-size (2½-inch) muffin cups.

2. Pour contents of jar into large bowl. Combine buttermilk, butter, eggs and vanilla in small bowl until blended; stir into jar mixture just until moistened. Spoon evenly into prepared muffin cups, filling about ⅔ full.

3. Bake 16 to 18 minutes or until toothpick inserted in centers comes out clean. Cool in pans on wire racks 5 minutes; remove from pans and cool 10 minutes on wire racks.

Makes 18 muffins

White Chocolate Chunk Muffins

1 jar White Chocolate Chunk
Muffin Mix
1⅓ cups buttermilk

6 tablespoons butter, melted
2 eggs, beaten
1½ teaspoons vanilla

1. Preheat oven to 400°F. Grease or paper-line 18 regular-size (2½-inch) muffin cups.

2. Pour contents of jar into large bowl. Combine buttermilk, butter, eggs and vanilla in small bowl until blended; stir into jar mixture just until moistened. Spoon evenly into prepared muffin cups, filling about ⅔ full.

3. Bake 16 to 18 minutes or until toothpick inserted in centers comes out clean. Cool in pans on wire racks 5 minutes; remove from pans and cool 10 minutes on wire racks.

Makes 18 muffins

White Chocolate Chunk Muffins

1 jar White Chocolate Chunk
Muffin Mix
1⅓ cups buttermilk

6 tablespoons butter, melted
2 eggs, beaten
1½ teaspoons vanilla

1. Preheat oven to 400°F. Grease or paper-line 18 regular-size (2½-inch) muffin cups.

2. Pour contents of jar into large bowl. Combine buttermilk, butter, eggs and vanilla in small bowl until blended; stir into jar mixture just until moistened. Spoon evenly into prepared muffin cups, filling about ⅔ full.

3. Bake 16 to 18 minutes or until toothpick inserted in centers comes out clean. Cool in pans on wire racks 5 minutes; remove from pans and cool 10 minutes on wire racks.

Makes 18 muffins

Cranberry Pecan Muffin Mix

1¾ cups all-purpose flour
1 cup dried cranberries
¾ cup chopped pecans
½ cup packed light brown sugar
2½ teaspoons baking powder
½ teaspoon salt

1. Layer ingredients attractively in any order into 1-quart food storage jar with tight-fitting lid. Pack ingredients down slightly before adding another layer.

2. Cover top of jar with fabric; attach gift tag with raffia or ribbon.

Makes one 1-quart jar

Cranberry Pecan Muffins

  1 jar Cranberry Pecan Muffin Mix
¾ cup milk
¼ cup butter, melted
  1 egg, beaten

1. Preheat oven to 400°F. Grease or paper-line 12 regular-size (2½-inch) muffin cups.

2. Pour contents of jar into large bowl. Combine milk, butter and egg in small bowl until blended; stir into jar mixture just until moistened. Spoon evenly into prepared muffin cups.

3. Bake 16 to 18 minutes or until toothpick inserted in centers comes out clean. Cool in pan on wire rack 5 minutes; remove from pan and cool completely on wire rack.   *Makes 12 muffins*

Cranberry Pecan Muffins

1 jar Cranberry Pecan Muffin Mix
¾ cup milk

¼ cup butter, melted
1 egg, beaten

1. Preheat oven to 400°F. Grease or paper-line 12 regular-size (2½-inch) muffin cups.

2. Pour contents of jar into large bowl. Combine milk, butter and egg in small bowl until blended; stir into jar mixture just until moistened. Spoon evenly into prepared muffin cups.

3. Bake 14 to 16 minutes or until toothpick inserted in centers comes out clean. Cool in pan on wire rack 5 minutes; remove from pan and cool completely on wire rack.

Makes 12 muffins

Cranberry Pecan Muffins

1 jar Cranberry Pecan Muffin Mix
¾ cup milk

¼ cup butter, melted
1 egg, beaten

1. Preheat oven to 400°F. Grease or paper-line 12 regular-size (2½-inch) muffin cups.

2. Pour contents of jar into large bowl. Combine milk, butter and egg in small bowl until blended; stir into jar mixture just until moistened. Spoon evenly into prepared muffin cups.

3. Bake 14 to 16 minutes or until toothpick inserted in centers comes out clean. Cool in pan on wire rack 5 minutes; remove from pan and cool completely on wire rack.

Makes 12 muffins

Cranberry Pecan Muffins

1 jar Cranberry Pecan Muffin Mix
¾ cup milk

¼ cup butter, melted
1 egg, beaten

1. Preheat oven to 400°F. Grease or paper-line 12 regular-size (2½-inch) muffin cups.

2. Pour contents of jar into large bowl. Combine milk, butter and egg in small bowl until blended; stir into jar mixture just until moistened. Spoon evenly into prepared muffin cups.

3. Bake 14 to 16 minutes or until toothpick inserted in centers comes out clean. Cool in pan on wire rack 5 minutes; remove from pan and cool completely on wire rack.

Makes 12 muffins

Cranberry Pecan Muffins

1 jar Cranberry Pecan Muffin Mix   ¼ cup butter, melted
¾ cup milk   1 egg, beaten

1. Preheat oven to 400°F. Grease or paper-line 12 regular-size (2½-inch) muffin cups.

2. Pour contents of jar into large bowl. Combine milk, butter and egg in small bowl until blended; stir into jar mixture just until moistened. Spoon evenly into prepared muffin cups.

3. Bake 14 to 16 minutes or until toothpick inserted in centers comes out clean. Cool in pan on wire rack 5 minutes; remove from pan and cool completely on wire rack.

Makes 12 muffins

Cranberry Pecan Muffins

1 jar Cranberry Pecan Muffin Mix   ¼ cup butter, melted
¾ cup milk   1 egg, beaten

1. Preheat oven to 400°F. Grease or paper-line 12 regular-size (2½-inch) muffin cups.

2. Pour contents of jar into large bowl. Combine milk, butter and egg in small bowl until blended; stir into jar mixture just until moistened. Spoon evenly into prepared muffin cups.

3. Bake 14 to 16 minutes or until toothpick inserted in centers comes out clean. Cool in pan on wire rack 5 minutes; remove from pan and cool completely on wire rack.

Makes 12 muffins

Cranberry Pecan Muffins

1 jar Cranberry Pecan Muffin Mix   ¼ cup butter, melted
¾ cup milk   1 egg, beaten

1. Preheat oven to 400°F. Grease or paper-line 12 regular-size (2½-inch) muffin cups.

2. Pour contents of jar into large bowl. Combine milk, butter and egg in small bowl until blended; stir into jar mixture just until moistened. Spoon evenly into prepared muffin cups.

3. Bake 14 to 16 minutes or until toothpick inserted in centers comes out clean. Cool in pan on wire rack 5 minutes; remove from pan and cool completely on wire rack.

Makes 12 muffins

Fruity Gingerbread Muffin Mix

1¾ cups all-purpose flour

1 cup chopped dried mixed fruit bits

1 cup chopped nuts

⅓ cup sugar

2 teaspoons baking powder

¾ teaspoon ground ginger

¼ teaspoon salt

¼ teaspoon baking soda

¼ teaspoon ground cinnamon

1. Layer ingredients attractively in any order into 1-quart food storage jar with tight-fitting lid. Pack ingredients down slightly before adding another layer.

2. Cover top of jar with fabric; attach gift tag with raffia or ribbon.

Makes one 1-quart jar

Fruity Gingerbread Muffins

1 jar Fruity Gingerbread Muffin Mix
½ cup milk
⅓ cup vegetable oil
¼ cup light molasses
1 egg

1. Preheat oven to 375°F. Grease or paper-line 12 regular-size (2½-inch) muffin cups.

2. Pour contents of jar into large bowl. Combine milk, oil, molasses and egg in medium bowl; stir into jar mixture just until moistened. Spoon evenly into prepared muffin cups, filling ⅔ full.

3. Bake 15 to 18 minutes or until toothpick inserted in centers comes out clean. Remove from pan; cool on wire rack 10 minutes. Serve warm or cold.   *Makes 12 muffins*

Fruity Gingerbread Muffins

1 jar Fruity Gingerbread Muffin Mix   ¼ cup light molasses
½ cup milk   1 egg
⅓ cup vegetable oil

1. Preheat oven to 375°F. Grease or paper-line 12 regular-size (2½-inch) muffin cups.

2. Pour contents of jar into large bowl. Combine milk, oil, molasses and egg in medium bowl; stir into jar mixture just until moistened. Spoon evenly into prepared muffin cups, filling ⅔ full.

3. Bake 15 to 18 minutes or until toothpick inserted in centers comes out clean. Remove from pan; cool on wire rack 10 minutes. Serve warm or cold.   *Makes 12 muffins*

Fruity Gingerbread Muffins

1 jar Fruity Gingerbread Muffin Mix   ¼ cup light molasses
½ cup milk   1 egg
⅓ cup vegetable oil

1. Preheat oven to 375°F. Grease or paper-line 12 regular-size (2½-inch) muffin cups.

2. Pour contents of jar into large bowl. Combine milk, oil, molasses and egg in medium bowl; stir into jar mixture just until moistened. Spoon evenly into prepared muffin cups, filling ⅔ full.

3. Bake 15 to 18 minutes or until toothpick inserted in centers comes out clean. Remove from pan; cool on wire rack 10 minutes. Serve warm or cold.   *Makes 12 muffins*

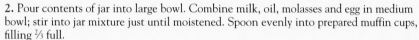

Fruity Gingerbread Muffins

1 jar Fruity Gingerbread Muffin Mix   ¼ cup light molasses
½ cup milk   1 egg
⅓ cup vegetable oil

1. Preheat oven to 375°F. Grease or paper-line 12 regular-size (2½-inch) muffin cups.

2. Pour contents of jar into large bowl. Combine milk, oil, molasses and egg in medium bowl; stir into jar mixture just until moistened. Spoon evenly into prepared muffin cups, filling ⅔ full.

3. Bake 15 to 18 minutes or until toothpick inserted in centers comes out clean. Remove from pan; cool on wire rack 10 minutes. Serve warm or cold.   *Makes 12 muffins*

Fruity Gingerbread Muffins

1 jar Fruity Gingerbread Muffin Mix   ¼ cup light molasses
½ cup milk   1 egg
⅓ cup vegetable oil

1. Preheat oven to 375°F. Grease or paper-line 12 regular-size (2½-inch) muffin cups.

2. Pour contents of jar into large bowl. Combine milk, oil, molasses and egg in medium bowl; stir into jar mixture just until moistened. Spoon evenly into prepared muffin cups, filling ⅔ full.

3. Bake 15 to 18 minutes or until toothpick inserted in centers comes out clean. Remove from pan; cool on wire rack 10 minutes. Serve warm or cold.   *Makes 12 muffins*

Fruity Gingerbread Muffins

1 jar Fruity Gingerbread Muffin Mix   ¼ cup light molasses
½ cup milk   1 egg
⅓ cup vegetable oil

1. Preheat oven to 375°F. Grease or paper-line 12 regular-size (2½-inch) muffin cups.

2. Pour contents of jar into large bowl. Combine milk, oil, molasses and egg in medium bowl; stir into jar mixture just until moistened. Spoon evenly into prepared muffin cups, filling ⅔ full.

3. Bake 15 to 18 minutes or until toothpick inserted in centers comes out clean. Remove from pan; cool on wire rack 10 minutes. Serve warm or cold.   *Makes 12 muffins*

Fruity Gingerbread Muffins

1 jar Fruity Gingerbread Muffin Mix   ¼ cup light molasses
½ cup milk   1 egg
⅓ cup vegetable oil

1. Preheat oven to 375°F. Grease or paper-line 12 regular-size (2½-inch) muffin cups.

2. Pour contents of jar into large bowl. Combine milk, oil, molasses and egg in medium bowl; stir into jar mixture just until moistened. Spoon evenly into prepared muffin cups, filling ⅔ full.

3. Bake 15 to 18 minutes or until toothpick inserted in centers comes out clean. Remove from pan; cool on wire rack 10 minutes. Serve warm or cold.   *Makes 12 muffins*

English-Style Scone Mix

    3 cups all-purpose flour
    ¾ cup golden raisins
    ¾ cup finely chopped pitted dates
    1 tablespoon baking powder
    ¼ teaspoon salt

1. Layer ingredients attractively in any order into 1-quart food storage jar with tight-fitting lid.

2. Cover top of jar with fabric; attach gift tag with raffia or ribbon.

Makes one 1-quart jar

English-Style Scones

1 jar English-Style Scone Mix
6 tablespoons cold butter
4 eggs, divided
¾ cup heavy cream
2 teaspoons vanilla
1 teaspoon water

1. Preheat oven to 375°F. Grease two cookie sheets.

2. Pour contents of jar into large bowl. Add butter; blend with pastry blender or two knives until mixture resembles coarse crumbs. Beat 3 eggs, cream and vanilla in small bowl. Add to flour mixture; mix just until ingredients are moistened. Knead dough several times on lightly floured surface. Divide dough in half; place each half on prepared cookie sheet and pat into 6-inch circle (about 1 inch thick).

3. With sharp, wet knife, gently score each circle of dough into six wedges, cutting ¾ of the way into dough. Beat remaining egg with water; brush lightly over dough. Bake 18 to 20 minutes or until golden brown. Cool 5 minutes on wire rack. Cut into wedges. Serve warm with marmalade and whipped cream.

Makes 12 scones

English-Style Scones

1 jar English-Style Scone Mix	¾ cup heavy cream
6 tablespoons cold butter	2 teaspoons vanilla
4 eggs, divided	1 teaspoon water

1. Preheat oven to 375°F. Grease two cookie sheets.

2. Pour contents of jar into large bowl. Add butter; blend with pastry blender or two knives until mixture resembles coarse crumbs. Beat 3 eggs, cream and vanilla in small bowl. Add to flour mixture; mix just until ingredients are moistened. Knead dough several times on lightly floured surface. Divide dough in half; place each half on prepared cookie sheet and pat into 6-inch circle (about 1 inch thick).

3. With sharp, wet knife, gently score each circle of dough into six wedges, cutting ¼ of the way into dough. Beat remaining egg with water; brush lightly over dough. Bake 18 to 20 minutes or until golden brown. Cool 5 minutes on wire rack. Cut into wedges. Serve warm with marmalade and whipped cream. *Makes 12 scones*

English-Style Scones

1 jar English-Style Scone Mix	¾ cup heavy cream
6 tablespoons cold butter	2 teaspoons vanilla
4 eggs, divided	1 teaspoon water

1. Preheat oven to 375°F. Grease two cookie sheets.

2. Pour contents of jar into large bowl. Add butter; blend with pastry blender or two knives until mixture resembles coarse crumbs. Beat 3 eggs, cream and vanilla in small bowl. Add to flour mixture; mix just until ingredients are moistened. Knead dough several times on lightly floured surface. Divide dough in half; place each half on prepared cookie sheet and pat into 6-inch circle (about 1 inch thick).

3. With sharp, wet knife, gently score each circle of dough into six wedges, cutting ¼ of the way into dough. Beat remaining egg with water; brush lightly over dough. Bake 18 to 20 minutes or until golden brown. Cool 5 minutes on wire rack. Cut into wedges. Serve warm with marmalade and whipped cream. *Makes 12 scones*

English-Style Scones

1 jar English-Style Scone Mix	¾ cup heavy cream
6 tablespoons cold butter	2 teaspoons vanilla
4 eggs, divided	1 teaspoon water

1. Preheat oven to 375°F. Grease two cookie sheets.

2. Pour contents of jar into large bowl. Add butter; blend with pastry blender or two knives until mixture resembles coarse crumbs. Beat 3 eggs, cream and vanilla in small bowl. Add to flour mixture; mix just until ingredients are moistened. Knead dough several times on lightly floured surface. Divide dough in half; place each half on prepared cookie sheet and pat into 6-inch circle (about 1 inch thick).

3. With sharp, wet knife, gently score each circle of dough into six wedges, cutting ¼ of the way into dough. Beat remaining egg with water; brush lightly over dough. Bake 18 to 20 minutes or until golden brown. Cool 5 minutes on wire rack. Cut into wedges. Serve warm with marmalade and whipped cream. *Makes 12 scones*

English-Style Scones

1 jar English-Style Scone Mix	¾ cup heavy cream
6 tablespoons cold butter	2 teaspoons vanilla
4 eggs, divided	1 teaspoon water

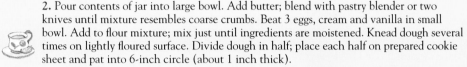

1. Preheat oven to 375°F. Grease two cookie sheets.

2. Pour contents of jar into large bowl. Add butter; blend with pastry blender or two knives until mixture resembles coarse crumbs. Beat 3 eggs, cream and vanilla in small bowl. Add to flour mixture; mix just until ingredients are moistened. Knead dough several times on lightly floured surface. Divide dough in half; place each half on prepared cookie sheet and pat into 6-inch circle (about 1 inch thick).

3. With sharp, wet knife, gently score each circle of dough into six wedges, cutting ¾ of the way into dough. Beat remaining egg with water; brush lightly over dough. Bake 18 to 20 minutes or until golden brown. Cool 5 minutes on wire rack. Cut into wedges. Serve warm with marmalade and whipped cream. *Makes 12 scones*

English-Style Scones

1 jar English-Style Scone Mix	¾ cup heavy cream
6 tablespoons cold butter	2 teaspoons vanilla
4 eggs, divided	1 teaspoon water

1. Preheat oven to 375°F. Grease two cookie sheets.

2. Pour contents of jar into large bowl. Add butter; blend with pastry blender or two knives until mixture resembles coarse crumbs. Beat 3 eggs, cream and vanilla in small bowl. Add to flour mixture; mix just until ingredients are moistened. Knead dough several times on lightly floured surface. Divide dough in half; place each half on prepared cookie sheet and pat into 6-inch circle (about 1 inch thick).

3. With sharp, wet knife, gently score each circle of dough into six wedges, cutting ¾ of the way into dough. Beat remaining egg with water; brush lightly over dough. Bake 18 to 20 minutes or until golden brown. Cool 5 minutes on wire rack. Cut into wedges. Serve warm with marmalade and whipped cream. *Makes 12 scones*

English-Style Scones

1 jar English-Style Scone Mix	¾ cup heavy cream
6 tablespoons cold butter	2 teaspoons vanilla
4 eggs, divided	1 teaspoon water

1. Preheat oven to 375°F. Grease two cookie sheets.

2. Pour contents of jar into large bowl. Add butter; blend with pastry blender or two knives until mixture resembles coarse crumbs. Beat 3 eggs, cream and vanilla in small bowl. Add to flour mixture; mix just until ingredients are moistened. Knead dough several times on lightly floured surface. Divide dough in half; place each half on prepared cookie sheet and pat into 6-inch circle (about 1 inch thick).

3. With sharp, wet knife, gently score each circle of dough into six wedges, cutting ¾ of the way into dough. Beat remaining egg with water; brush lightly over dough. Bake 18 to 20 minutes or until golden brown. Cool 5 minutes on wire rack. Cut into wedges. Serve warm with marmalade and whipped cream. *Makes 12 scones*

Toffee Delight Muffin Mix

3 cups all-purpose flour
1 package (8 ounces) chocolate-covered toffee bits
⅔ cup packed brown sugar
1 tablespoon baking powder
1 teaspoon baking soda
½ teaspoon salt

1. Layer ingredients attractively in any order into 1-quart food storage jar with tight-fitting lid. Pack ingredients down slightly before adding another layer.

2. Cover top of jar with fabric; attach gift tag with raffia or ribbon.

Makes one 1-quart jar

Toffee Delight Muffins

1 jar Toffee Delight Muffin Mix
1 cup milk
1 cup sour cream
6 tablespoons butter, melted
2 eggs
2 teaspoons vanilla

1. Preheat oven to 400°F. Grease or paper-line 24 regular-size (2½-inch) muffin cups.

2. Pour contents of jar into large bowl. Combine milk, sour cream, butter, eggs and vanilla in small bowl until blended; stir into jar mixture just until moistened. Spoon evenly into prepared muffin cups, filling ⅔ full.

3. Bake 16 to 18 minutes or until toothpick inserted in centers comes out clean. Remove from pans and cool 10 minutes on wire racks. Serve warm or cool completely.   *Makes 24 muffins*

Toffee Delight Muffins

1 jar Toffee Delight Muffin Mix
1 cup milk
1 cup sour cream

6 tablespoons butter, melted
2 eggs
2 teaspoons vanilla

1. Preheat oven to 400°F. Grease or paper-line 24 regular-size (2½-inch) muffin cups.

2. Pour contents of jar into large bowl. Combine milk, sour cream, butter, eggs and vanilla in small bowl until blended; stir into jar mixture just until moistened. Spoon evenly into prepared muffin cups, filling ⅔ full.

3. Bake 16 to 18 minutes or until toothpick inserted in centers comes out clean. Remove from pans and cool 10 minutes on wire racks. Serve warm or cool completely.

Makes 24 muffins

Toffee Delight Muffins

1 jar Toffee Delight Muffin Mix
1 cup milk
1 cup sour cream

6 tablespoons butter, melted
2 eggs
2 teaspoons vanilla

1. Preheat oven to 400°F. Grease or paper-line 24 regular-size (2½-inch) muffin cups.

2. Pour contents of jar into large bowl. Combine milk, sour cream, butter, eggs and vanilla in small bowl until blended; stir into jar mixture just until moistened. Spoon evenly into prepared muffin cups, filling ⅔ full.

3. Bake 16 to 18 minutes or until toothpick inserted in centers comes out clean. Remove from pans and cool 10 minutes on wire racks. Serve warm or cool completely.

Makes 24 muffins

Toffee Delight Muffins

1 jar Toffee Delight Muffin Mix
1 cup milk
1 cup sour cream

6 tablespoons butter, melted
2 eggs
2 teaspoons vanilla

1. Preheat oven to 400°F. Grease or paper-line 24 regular-size (2½-inch) muffin cups.

2. Pour contents of jar into large bowl. Combine milk, sour cream, butter, eggs and vanilla in small bowl until blended; stir into jar mixture just until moistened. Spoon evenly into prepared muffin cups, filling ⅔ full.

3. Bake 16 to 18 minutes or until toothpick inserted in centers comes out clean. Remove from pans and cool 10 minutes on wire racks. Serve warm or cool completely.

Makes 24 muffins

Toffee Delight Muffins

1 jar Toffee Delight Muffin Mix
1 cup milk
1 cup sour cream

6 tablespoons butter, melted
2 eggs
2 teaspoons vanilla

1. Preheat oven to 400°F. Grease or paper-line 24 regular-size (2½-inch) muffin cups.

2. Pour contents of jar into large bowl. Combine milk, sour cream, butter, eggs and vanilla in small bowl until blended; stir into jar mixture just until moistened. Spoon evenly into prepared muffin cups, filling ⅔ full.

3. Bake 16 to 18 minutes or until toothpick inserted in centers comes out clean. Remove from pans and cool 10 minutes on wire racks. Serve warm or cool completely.

Makes 24 muffins

Toffee Delight Muffins

1 jar Toffee Delight Muffin Mix
1 cup milk
1 cup sour cream

6 tablespoons butter, melted
2 eggs
2 teaspoons vanilla

1. Preheat oven to 400°F. Grease or paper-line 24 regular-size (2½-inch) muffin cups.

2. Pour contents of jar into large bowl. Combine milk, sour cream, butter, eggs and vanilla in small bowl until blended; stir into jar mixture just until moistened. Spoon evenly into prepared muffin cups, filling ⅔ full.

3. Bake 16 to 18 minutes or until toothpick inserted in centers comes out clean. Remove from pans and cool 10 minutes on wire racks. Serve warm or cool completely.

Makes 24 muffins

Toffee Delight Muffins

1 jar Toffee Delight Muffin Mix
1 cup milk
1 cup sour cream

6 tablespoons butter, melted
2 eggs
2 teaspoons vanilla

1. Preheat oven to 400°F. Grease or paper-line 24 regular-size (2½-inch) muffin cups.

2. Pour contents of jar into large bowl. Combine milk, sour cream, butter, eggs and vanilla in small bowl until blended; stir into jar mixture just until moistened. Spoon evenly into prepared muffin cups, filling ⅔ full.

3. Bake 16 to 18 minutes or until toothpick inserted in centers comes out clean. Remove from pans and cool 10 minutes on wire racks. Serve warm or cool completely.

Makes 24 muffins

Chocolate Macadamia Nut Muffin Mix

2 cups all-purpose flour
1 cup sugar
1 cup chocolate chips
½ cup coarsely chopped macadamia nuts
¼ cup unsweetened cocoa powder
1½ teaspoons baking soda
½ teaspoon salt

1. Layer ingredients attractively in any order into 1-quart food storage jar with tight-fitting lid. Pack ingredients down slightly before adding another layer.

2. Cover top of jar with fabric; attach gift tag with raffia or ribbon.

Makes one 1-quart jar

Chocolate Macadamia Nut Muffins

1 jar Chocolate Macadamia Nut Muffin Mix
1 cup buttermilk
⅓ cup butter, melted
2 eggs
1½ teaspoons vanilla
   Powdered sugar (optional)

1. Preheat oven to 400°F. Grease or paper-line 18 regular-size (2½-inch) muffin cups.

2. Pour contents of jar into large bowl. Combine buttermilk, butter, eggs and vanilla in small bowl until blended; stir into jar mixture just until moistened. Spoon evenly into prepared muffin cups.

3. Bake 13 to 17 minutes or until toothpick inserted in centers comes out clean. Cool in pans on wire racks 5 minutes; remove from pans and cool completely on wire racks. Sprinkle with powdered sugar, if desired.   *Makes 18 muffins*

Chocolate Macadamia Nut Muffins

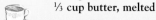

1 jar Chocolate Macadamia Nut
    Muffin Mix
1 cup buttermilk
⅓ cup butter, melted

2 eggs
1½ teaspoons vanilla
Powdered sugar (optional)

1. Preheat oven to 400°F. Grease or paper-line 18 regular-size (2½-inch) muffin cups.

2. Pour contents of jar into large bowl. Combine buttermilk, butter, eggs and vanilla in small bowl until blended; stir into jar mixture just until moistened. Spoon evenly into prepared muffin cups.

3. Bake 13 to 17 minutes or until toothpick inserted in centers comes out clean. Cool in pans on wire racks 5 minutes; remove from pans and cool completely on wire racks. Sprinkle with powdered sugar, if desired. *Makes 18 muffins*

Chocolate Macadamia Nut Muffins

1 jar Chocolate Macadamia Nut
    Muffin Mix
1 cup buttermilk
⅓ cup butter, melted

2 eggs
1½ teaspoons vanilla
Powdered sugar (optional)

1. Preheat oven to 400°F. Grease or paper-line 18 regular-size (2½-inch) muffin cups.

2. Pour contents of jar into large bowl. Combine buttermilk, butter, eggs and vanilla in small bowl until blended; stir into jar mixture just until moistened. Spoon evenly into prepared muffin cups.

3. Bake 13 to 17 minutes or until toothpick inserted in centers comes out clean. Cool in pans on wire racks 5 minutes; remove from pans and cool completely on wire racks. Sprinkle with powdered sugar, if desired. *Makes 18 muffins*

Chocolate Macadamia Nut Muffins

1 jar Chocolate Macadamia Nut
    Muffin Mix
1 cup buttermilk
⅓ cup butter, melted

2 eggs
1½ teaspoons vanilla
Powdered sugar (optional)

1. Preheat oven to 400°F. Grease or paper-line 18 regular-size (2½-inch) muffin cups.

2. Pour contents of jar into large bowl. Combine buttermilk, butter, eggs and vanilla in small bowl until blended; stir into jar mixture just until moistened. Spoon evenly into prepared muffin cups.

3. Bake 13 to 17 minutes or until toothpick inserted in centers comes out clean. Cool in pans on wire racks 5 minutes; remove from pans and cool completely on wire racks. Sprinkle with powdered sugar, if desired. *Makes 18 muffins*

Chocolate Macadamia Nut Muffins

1 jar Chocolate Macadamia Nut
    Muffin Mix
1 cup buttermilk
⅓ cup butter, melted

2 eggs
1½ teaspoons vanilla
Powdered sugar (optional)

1. Preheat oven to 400°F. Grease or paper-line 18 regular-size (2½-inch) muffin cups.

2. Pour contents of jar into large bowl. Combine buttermilk, butter, eggs and vanilla in small bowl until blended; stir into jar mixture just until moistened. Spoon evenly into prepared muffin cups.

3. Bake 13 to 17 minutes or until toothpick inserted in centers comes out clean. Cool in pans on wire racks 5 minutes; remove from pans and cool completely on wire racks. Sprinkle with powdered sugar, if desired. *Makes 18 muffins*

Chocolate Macadamia Nut Muffins

1 jar Chocolate Macadamia Nut
    Muffin Mix
1 cup buttermilk
⅓ cup butter, melted

2 eggs
1½ teaspoons vanilla
Powdered sugar (optional)

1. Preheat oven to 400°F. Grease or paper-line 18 regular-size (2½-inch) muffin cups.

2. Pour contents of jar into large bowl. Combine buttermilk, butter, eggs and vanilla in small bowl until blended; stir into jar mixture just until moistened. Spoon evenly into prepared muffin cups.

3. Bake 13 to 17 minutes or until toothpick inserted in centers comes out clean. Cool in pans on wire racks 5 minutes; remove from pans and cool completely on wire racks. Sprinkle with powdered sugar, if desired. *Makes 18 muffins*

Chocolate Macadamia Nut Muffins

1 jar Chocolate Macadamia Nut
    Muffin Mix
1 cup buttermilk
⅓ cup butter, melted

2 eggs
1½ teaspoons vanilla
Powdered sugar (optional)

1. Preheat oven to 400°F. Grease or paper-line 18 regular-size (2½-inch) muffin cups.

2. Pour contents of jar into large bowl. Combine buttermilk, butter, eggs and vanilla in small bowl until blended; stir into jar mixture just until moistened. Spoon evenly into prepared muffin cups.

3. Bake 13 to 17 minutes or until toothpick inserted in centers comes out clean. Cool in pans on wire racks 5 minutes; remove from pans and cool completely on wire racks. Sprinkle with powdered sugar, if desired. *Makes 18 muffins*

Granola Spice Muffin Mix

  3 cups all-purpose flour
  1 cup granola
  ¾ cup sugar
  ½ cup raisins
  1 tablespoon baking powder
  1 teaspoon ground cinnamon
  ½ teaspoon salt
  ¼ teaspoon ground nutmeg
  ⅛ teaspoon ground allspice

1. Layer ingredients attractively in any order into 1-quart food storage jar with tight-fitting lid. Pack ingredients down slightly before adding another layer.

2. Cover top of jar with fabric; attach gift tag with raffia or ribbon.

Makes one 1-quart jar

Granola Spice Muffins

- 1 jar Granola Spice Muffin Mix
- 1½ cups milk
- 6 tablespoons vegetable oil
- 2 eggs

1. Preheat oven to 400°F. Grease or paper-line 18 regular-size (2½-inch) muffin cups.

2. Pour contents of jar into large bowl. Combine milk, oil and eggs in small bowl until blended; stir into jar mixture just until moistened. Spoon evenly into prepared muffin cups.

3. Bake 15 to 17 minutes or until toothpick inserted in centers comes out clean. Remove from pans and cool on wire racks.

Makes 18 muffins

Granola Spice Muffins

1 jar Granola Spice Muffin Mix   6 tablespoons vegetable oil
1½ cups milk   2 eggs

1. Preheat oven to 400°F. Grease or paper-line 18 regular-size (2½-inch) muffin cups.

2. Pour contents of jar into large bowl. Combine milk, oil and eggs in small bowl until blended; stir into jar mixture just until moistened. Spoon evenly into prepared muffin cups.

3. Bake 15 to 17 minutes or until toothpick inserted in centers comes out clean. Remove from pans and cool on wire racks.   *Makes 18 muffins*

Granola Spice Muffins

1 jar Granola Spice Muffin Mix   6 tablespoons vegetable oil
1½ cups milk   2 eggs

1. Preheat oven to 400°F. Grease or paper-line 18 regular-size (2½-inch) muffin cups.

2. Pour contents of jar into large bowl. Combine milk, oil and eggs in small bowl until blended; stir into jar mixture just until moistened. Spoon evenly into prepared muffin cups.

3. Bake 15 to 17 minutes or until toothpick inserted in centers comes out clean. Remove from pans and cool on wire racks.   *Makes 18 muffins*

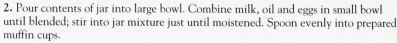
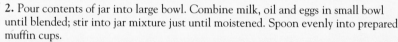

Granola Spice Muffins

1 jar Granola Spice Muffin Mix   6 tablespoons vegetable oil
1½ cups milk   2 eggs

1. Preheat oven to 400°F. Grease or paper-line 18 regular-size (2½-inch) muffin cups.

2. Pour contents of jar into large bowl. Combine milk, oil and eggs in small bowl until blended; stir into jar mixture just until moistened. Spoon evenly into prepared muffin cups.

3. Bake 15 to 17 minutes or until toothpick inserted in centers comes out clean. Remove from pans and cool on wire racks.   *Makes 18 muffins*

Granola Spice Muffins

1 jar Granola Spice Muffin Mix
1½ cups milk

6 tablespoons vegetable oil
2 eggs

1. Preheat oven to 400°F. Grease or paper-line 18 regular-size (2½-inch) muffin cups.

2. Pour contents of jar into large bowl. Combine milk, oil and eggs in small bowl until blended; stir into jar mixture just until moistened. Spoon evenly into prepared muffin cups.

3. Bake 15 to 17 minutes or until toothpick inserted in centers comes out clean. Remove from pans and cool on wire racks. *Makes 18 muffins*

Granola Spice Muffins

1 jar Granola Spice Muffin Mix
1½ cups milk

6 tablespoons vegetable oil
2 eggs

1. Preheat oven to 400°F. Grease or paper-line 18 regular-size (2½-inch) muffin cups.

2. Pour contents of jar into large bowl. Combine milk, oil and eggs in small bowl until blended; stir into jar mixture just until moistened. Spoon evenly into prepared muffin cups.

3. Bake 15 to 17 minutes or until toothpick inserted in centers comes out clean. Remove from pans and cool on wire racks. *Makes 18 muffins*

Granola Spice Muffins

1 jar Granola Spice Muffin Mix
1½ cups milk

6 tablespoons vegetable oil
2 eggs

1. Preheat oven to 400°F. Grease or paper-line 18 regular-size (2½-inch) muffin cups.

2. Pour contents of jar into large bowl. Combine milk, oil and eggs in small bowl until blended; stir into jar mixture just until moistened. Spoon evenly into prepared muffin cups.

3. Bake 15 to 17 minutes or until toothpick inserted in centers comes out clean. Remove from pans and cool on wire racks. *Makes 18 muffins*

Currant Scone Mix

3 cups all-purpose flour
½ cup sugar
2 teaspoons baking powder
½ teaspoon salt
½ teaspoon baking soda
1 cup currants

1. Layer ingredients attractively in any order into 1-quart food storage jar with tight-fitting lid.

2. Cover top of jar with fabric; attach gift tag with raffia or ribbon.

Makes one 1-quart jar

Currant Scones

1 jar Currant Scone Mix
¾ cup chilled butter, cut into small pieces
1 cup buttermilk
1 tablespoon grated fresh orange peel (optional)

1. Preheat oven to 425°F. Lightly grease two cookie sheets.

2. Pour contents of jar into large bowl. Cut in butter with pastry blender or two knives until mixture resembles coarse crumbs. Stir in buttermilk and orange peel. Stir until mixture forms soft dough that clings together. (Dough will be tacky.)

3. Lightly flour hands; divide dough in half and shape each half into a ball. Pat each ball into 8-inch circle on prepared cookie sheets. Score each circle into 8 wedges with floured knife, cutting about ¾ of the way into dough. Bake 16 to 18 minutes or until lightly browned. Cut into wedges; serve warm. *Makes 16 scones*

Currant Scones

1 jar Currant Scone Mix
¾ cup chilled butter, cut into small pieces

1 cup buttermilk
1 tablespoon grated fresh orange peel (optional)

1. Preheat oven to 425°F. Lightly grease two cookie sheets.

2. Pour contents of jar into large bowl. Cut in butter with pastry blender or two knives until mixture resembles coarse crumbs. Stir in buttermilk and orange peel. Stir until mixture forms soft dough that clings together. (Dough will be tacky.)

3. Lightly flour hands; divide dough in half and shape each half into a ball. Pat each ball into 8-inch circle on prepared cookie sheets. Score each circle into 8 wedges with floured knife, cutting about ¾ of the way into dough. Bake 16 to 18 minutes or until lightly browned. Cut into wedges; serve warm.
Makes 16 scones

Currant Scones

1 jar Currant Scone Mix
¾ cup chilled butter, cut into small pieces

1 cup buttermilk
1 tablespoon grated fresh orange peel (optional)

1. Preheat oven to 425°F. Lightly grease two cookie sheets.

2. Pour contents of jar into large bowl. Cut in butter with pastry blender or two knives until mixture resembles coarse crumbs. Stir in buttermilk and orange peel. Stir until mixture forms soft dough that clings together. (Dough will be tacky.)

3. Lightly flour hands; divide dough in half and shape each half into a ball. Pat each ball into 8-inch circle on prepared cookie sheets. Score each circle into 8 wedges with floured knife, cutting about ¾ of the way into dough. Bake 16 to 18 minutes or until lightly browned. Cut into wedges; serve warm.
Makes 16 scones

Currant Scones

1 jar Currant Scone Mix
¾ cup chilled butter, cut into small pieces

1 cup buttermilk
1 tablespoon grated fresh orange peel (optional)

1. Preheat oven to 425°F. Lightly grease two cookie sheets.

2. Pour contents of jar into large bowl. Cut in butter with pastry blender or two knives until mixture resembles coarse crumbs. Stir in buttermilk and orange peel. Stir until mixture forms soft dough that clings together. (Dough will be tacky.)

3. Lightly flour hands; divide dough in half and shape each half into a ball. Pat each ball into 8-inch circle on prepared cookie sheets. Score each circle into 8 wedges with floured knife, cutting about ¾ of the way into dough. Bake 16 to 18 minutes or until lightly browned. Cut into wedges; serve warm.
Makes 16 scones

Currant Scones

1 jar Currant Scone Mix
¾ cup chilled butter, cut into
　　small pieces

1 cup buttermilk
1 tablespoon grated fresh orange peel
　　(optional)

1. Preheat oven to 425°F. Lightly grease two cookie sheets.

2. Pour contents of jar into large bowl. Cut in butter with pastry blender or two knives until mixture resembles coarse crumbs. Stir in buttermilk and orange peel. Stir until mixture forms soft dough that clings together. (Dough will be tacky.)

3. Lightly flour hands; divide dough in half and shape each half into a ball. Pat each ball into 8-inch circle on prepared cookie sheets. Score each circle into 8 wedges with floured knife, cutting about ¼ of the way into dough. Bake 16 to 18 minutes or until lightly browned. Cut into wedges; serve warm. *Makes 16 scones*

Currant Scones

1 jar Currant Scone Mix
¾ cup chilled butter, cut into
　　small pieces

1 cup buttermilk
1 tablespoon grated fresh orange peel
　　(optional)

1. Preheat oven to 425°F. Lightly grease two cookie sheets.

2. Pour contents of jar into large bowl. Cut in butter with pastry blender or two knives until mixture resembles coarse crumbs. Stir in buttermilk and orange peel. Stir until mixture forms soft dough that clings together. (Dough will be tacky.)

3. Lightly flour hands; divide dough in half and shape each half into a ball. Pat each ball into 8-inch circle on prepared cookie sheets. Score each circle into 8 wedges with floured knife, cutting about ¼ of the way into dough. Bake 16 to 18 minutes or until lightly browned. Cut into wedges; serve warm. *Makes 16 scones*

Currant Scones

1 jar Currant Scone Mix
¾ cup chilled butter, cut into
　　small pieces

1 cup buttermilk
1 tablespoon grated fresh orange peel
　　(optional)

1. Preheat oven to 425°F. Lightly grease two cookie sheets.

2. Pour contents of jar into large bowl. Cut in butter with pastry blender or two knives until mixture resembles coarse crumbs. Stir in buttermilk and orange peel. Stir until mixture forms soft dough that clings together. (Dough will be tacky.)

3. Lightly flour hands; divide dough in half and shape each half into a ball. Pat each ball into 8-inch circle on prepared cookie sheets. Score each circle into 8 wedges with floured knife, cutting about ¼ of the way into dough. Bake 16 to 18 minutes or until lightly browned. Cut into wedges; serve warm. *Makes 16 scones*

Strawberry Muffin Mix

2 cups all-purpose flour
1½ cups uncooked old-fashioned oats
¾ cup sugar
3½ teaspoons baking powder
½ teaspoon salt
½ teaspoon ground cinnamon

1. Layer ingredients attractively in any order into 1-quart food storage jar with tight-fitting lid. Pack ingredients down slightly before adding another layer.

2. Cover top of jar with fabric; attach gift tag with raffia or ribbon.

Makes one 1-quart jar

Strawberry Muffins

1 jar Strawberry Muffin Mix
1½ cups milk
¾ cup butter, melted
2 eggs, beaten
1½ teaspoons vanilla
2 cups chopped fresh or frozen strawberries (thaw and drain before using)

1. Preheat oven to 400°F. Grease or paper-line 18 regular-size (2½-inch) muffin cups.

2. Pour contents of jar into large bowl. Combine milk, butter, eggs and vanilla in small bowl until blended; stir into jar mixture just until moistened. Gently fold in strawberries. Spoon evenly into prepared muffin cups, filling almost full.

3. Bake 15 to 17 minutes or until toothpick inserted in centers comes out clean. Remove from pans and cool 10 minutes on wire racks. Serve warm or cool completely.   *Makes 18 muffins*

Strawberry Muffins

1 jar Strawberry Muffin Mix
1½ cups milk
¾ cup butter, melted
2 eggs, beaten

1½ teaspoons vanilla
2 cups chopped fresh or frozen
   strawberries (thaw and drain
   before using)

1. Preheat oven to 400°F. Grease or paper-line 18 regular-size (2½-inch) muffin cups.

2. Pour contents of jar into large bowl. Combine milk, butter, eggs and vanilla in small bowl until blended; stir into jar mixture just until moistened. Gently fold in stawberries. Spoon evenly into prepared muffin cups, filling almost full.

3. Bake 15 to 17 minutes or until toothpick inserted in centers comes out clean. Remove from pans and cool 10 minutes on wire racks. Serve warm or cool completely.

Makes 18 muffins

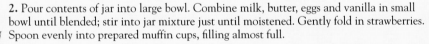

Strawberry Muffins

1 jar Strawberry Muffin Mix
1½ cups milk
¾ cup butter, melted
2 eggs, beaten

1½ teaspoons vanilla
2 cups chopped fresh or frozen
   strawberries (thaw and drain
   before using)

1. Preheat oven to 400°F. Grease or paper-line 18 regular-size (2½-inch) muffin cups.

2. Pour contents of jar into large bowl. Combine milk, butter, eggs and vanilla in small bowl until blended; stir into jar mixture just until moistened. Gently fold in strawberries. Spoon evenly into prepared muffin cups, filling almost full.

3. Bake 15 to 17 minutes or until toothpick inserted in centers comes out clean. Remove from pans and cool 10 minutes on wire racks. Serve warm or cool completely.

Makes 18 muffins

Strawberry Muffins

1 jar Strawberry Muffin Mix
1½ cups milk
¾ cup butter, melted
2 eggs, beaten

1½ teaspoons vanilla
2 cups chopped fresh or frozen
   strawberries (thaw and drain
   before using)

1. Preheat oven to 400°F. Grease or paper-line 18 regular-size (2½-inch) muffin cups.

2. Pour contents of jar into large bowl. Combine milk, butter, eggs and vanilla in small bowl until blended; stir into jar mixture just until moistened. Gently fold in strawberries. Spoon evenly into prepared muffin cups, filling almost full.

3. Bake 15 to 17 minutes or until toothpick inserted in centers comes out clean. Remove from pans and cool 10 minutes on wire racks. Serve warm or cool completely.

Makes 18 muffins

Strawberry Muffins

1 jar Strawberry Muffin Mix
1½ cups milk
¾ cup butter, melted
2 eggs, beaten

1½ teaspoons vanilla
2 cups chopped fresh or frozen
   strawberries (thaw and drain
   before using)

1. Preheat oven to 400°F. Grease or paper-line 18 regular-size (2½-inch) muffin cups.

2. Pour contents of jar into large bowl. Combine milk, butter, eggs and vanilla in small bowl until blended; stir into jar mixture just until moistened. Gently fold in stawberries. Spoon evenly into prepared muffin cups, filling almost full.

3. Bake 15 to 17 minutes or until toothpick inserted in centers comes out clean. Remove from pans and cool 10 minutes on wire racks. Serve warm or cool completely.

Makes 18 muffins

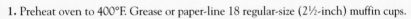

Strawberry Muffins

1 jar Strawberry Muffin Mix
1½ cups milk
¾ cup butter, melted
2 eggs, beaten

1½ teaspoons vanilla
2 cups chopped fresh or frozen
   strawberries (thaw and drain
   before using)

1. Preheat oven to 400°F. Grease or paper-line 18 regular-size (2½-inch) muffin cups.

2. Pour contents of jar into large bowl. Combine milk, butter, eggs and vanilla in small bowl until blended; stir into jar mixture just until moistened. Gently fold in strawberries. Spoon evenly into prepared muffin cups, filling almost full.

3. Bake 15 to 17 minutes or until toothpick inserted in centers comes out clean. Remove from pans and cool 10 minutes on wire racks. Serve warm or cool completely.

Makes 18 muffins

Strawberry Muffins

1 jar Strawberry Muffin Mix
1½ cups milk
¾ cup butter, melted
2 eggs, beaten

1½ teaspoons vanilla
2 cups chopped fresh or frozen
   strawberries (thaw and drain
   before using)

1. Preheat oven to 400°F. Grease or paper-line 18 regular-size (2½-inch) muffin cups.

2. Pour contents of jar into large bowl. Combine milk, butter, eggs and vanilla in small bowl until blended; stir into jar mixture just until moistened. Gently fold in strawberries. Spoon evenly into prepared muffin cups, filling almost full.

3. Bake 15 to 17 minutes or until toothpick inserted in centers comes out clean. Remove from pans and cool 10 minutes on wire racks. Serve warm or cool completely.

Makes 18 muffins

Apple Raisin Muffin Mix

1½ cups all-purpose flour
 1 cup chopped dried apples
⅔ cup packed brown sugar
½ cup uncooked old-fashioned oats
½ cup chopped walnuts
½ cup raisins
 1 tablespoon baking powder
 1 teaspoon ground cinnamon
½ teaspoon salt
⅛ teaspoon ground nutmeg
⅛ teaspoon ground ginger

1. Layer ingredients attractively in any order into 1-quart food storage jar with tight-fitting lid. Pack ingredients down slightly before adding another layer.

2. Cover top of jar with fabric; attach gift tag with raffia or ribbon.

Makes one 1-quart jar

Apple Raisin Muffins

1 jar Apple Raisin Muffin Mix
½ cup milk
½ cup butter, melted
2 eggs

1. Preheat oven to 400°F. Grease or paper-line 12 regular-size (2½-inch) muffin cups.

2. Pour contents of jar into large bowl. Combine milk, butter and eggs in small bowl until blended; stir into jar mixture just until moistened. Spoon evenly into prepared muffin cups, filling about ⅔ full.

3. Bake 15 to 17 minutes or until toothpick inserted in centers comes out clean. Remove from pan and cool on wire rack.

Makes 12 muffins

Apple Raisin Muffins

1 jar Apple Raisin Muffin Mix ½ cup butter, melted
½ cup milk 2 eggs

1. Preheat oven to 400°F. Grease or paper-line 12 regular-size (2½-inch) muffin cups.

2. Pour contents of jar into large bowl. Combine milk, butter and eggs in small bowl until blended; stir into jar mixture just until moistened. Spoon evenly into prepared muffin cups, filling about ⅔ full.

3. Bake 15 to 17 minutes or until toothpick inserted in centers comes out clean. Remove from pan and cool on wire rack. *Makes 12 muffins*

Apple Raisin Muffins

1 jar Apple Raisin Muffin Mix ½ cup butter, melted
½ cup milk 2 eggs

1. Preheat oven to 400°F. Grease or paper-line 12 regular-size (2½-inch) muffin cups.

2. Pour contents of jar into large bowl. Combine milk, butter and eggs in small bowl until blended; stir into jar mixture just until moistened. Spoon evenly into prepared muffin cups, filling about ⅔ full.

3. Bake 15 to 17 minutes or until toothpick inserted in centers comes out clean. Remove from pan and cool on wire rack. *Makes 12 muffins*

Apple Raisin Muffins

1 jar Apple Raisin Muffin Mix ½ cup butter, melted
½ cup milk 2 eggs

1. Preheat oven to 400°F. Grease or paper-line 12 regular-size (2½-inch) muffin cups.

2. Pour contents of jar into large bowl. Combine milk, butter and eggs in small bowl until blended; stir into jar mixture just until moistened. Spoon evenly into prepared muffin cups, filling about ⅔ full.

3. Bake 15 to 17 minutes or until toothpick inserted in centers comes out clean. Remove from pan and cool on wire rack. *Makes 12 muffins*

Apple Raisin Muffins

1 jar Apple Raisin Muffin Mix
½ **cup milk**

½ **cup butter, melted**
2 eggs

1. Preheat oven to 400°F. Grease or paper-line 12 regular-size (2½-inch) muffin cups.

2. Pour contents of jar into large bowl. Combine milk, butter and eggs in small bowl until blended; stir into jar mixture just until moistened. Spoon evenly into prepared muffin cups, filling about ⅔ full.

3. Bake 15 to 17 minutes or until toothpick inserted in centers comes out clean. Remove from pan and cool on wire rack. *Makes 12 muffins*

Apple Raisin Muffins

1 jar Apple Raisin Muffin Mix
½ **cup milk**

½ **cup butter, melted**
2 eggs

1. Preheat oven to 400°F. Grease or paper-line 12 regular-size (2½-inch) muffin cups.

2. Pour contents of jar into large bowl. Combine milk, butter and eggs in small bowl until blended; stir into jar mixture just until moistened. Spoon evenly into prepared muffin cups, filling about ⅔ full.

3. Bake 15 to 17 minutes or until toothpick inserted in centers comes out clean. Remove from pan and cool on wire rack. *Makes 12 muffins*

Apple Raisin Muffins

1 jar Apple Raisin Muffin Mix
½ **cup milk**

½ **cup butter, melted**
2 eggs

1. Preheat oven to 400°F. Grease or paper-line 12 regular-size (2½-inch) muffin cups.

2. Pour contents of jar into large bowl. Combine milk, butter and eggs in small bowl until blended; stir into jar mixture just until moistened. Spoon evenly into prepared muffin cups, filling about ⅔ full.

3. Bake 15 to 17 minutes or until toothpick inserted in centers comes out clean. Remove from pan and cool on wire rack. *Makes 12 muffins*

Notes

Notes